CONTENTS

PREFACE

... GO INTERVIEW THE P.M., KID...

It was September 1980. I clearly remember my first day on the job as a "cadet" journalist at radio 2CC in Canberra, Australia. "Double C" stood for "capital city", and this was the national capital's number one radio station, in a modern building on the outskirts of this still young metropolis. At the age of 20, I was employed as a cadet journalist, having been a presenter at a small country station for around ten months just before. My time had come.

Entering that open-plan newsroom for the first time, to the click-clack chorus of Remington typewriters and the ongoing bzzzz-bzzzz of the AAP wire service printer, the news director handed me a recording kit, along with the keys to a news car, and told me to head straight on out to interview the then prime minister, Malcolm Fraser. The PM was set to be using a small spade to ceremoniously "turn the first sod" on the construction site of the new parliament house on Capital Hill.

"What should I ask?", I inquired, with, no doubt, a slight look of panic in my eyes.

"You're the journalist now, mate. You work it out...", he replied.

That's called throwing the kid in at the deep end. I did come back later that day with a useable sound grab from the PM, and figured I had thus become a journalist (of sorts).

In the 1980's, commercial radio news in Australia – and probably in many other countries – was the "school of hard knocks". And while business could be cut-throat, the camaraderie was unlike anything I've seen in recent years. The desk editors, while they had little time to explain the finesse of writing, marked-up the typed pages, sometimes covering them with black lines and inserted text. It was nothing less than a great lesson each time I ripped a page from my typewriter and saw it placed on the news make-up board, which, for radio news, is very often indeed.

In those first years, I learned a hell of a lot. We all did then – as everything was analogue. Every time you looked at your news copy, you could see where you'd gone wrong and how to improve. Today, with digital workflows, no-one gets that feedback we had then, and that makes it much harder for young journalists to pick up the lessons. Many things have changed, some for the better, and, I fear, quite a few for the worse.

Over the years, I have also never ceased to be surprised by the poor quality of press releases that are produced by some of the world's top corporations and organisations in numerous fields, and even government agencies. It seems as though some PR writers have never even learned the basics when it comes to communicating. And it also appears the quality of what's being taught – or imparted – to journalists – is on the slide. Consequently, journalism in general is on the slide, too.

The onset of blogging and social media, along with increasing interference by those with a specific agenda has not just blurred, but destroyed the lines between news, propaganda, manipulation and rumour. So where is it all going? I do wonder, and I don't have an answer. I do however have a few tips for those who want to "get on" in the field of journalism – either hard news or commercial.

Flash-forward to today, and I've been working primarily over the past 20 years on trade publications, while keeping the hand in with other media. Working in the South of France for over 30 years now, my intern, Kira, a brilliant 20-year-old German undergraduate, quizzes me every day on the how's and why's of journalism, each time telling me, "But they don't teach us this practical stuff at uni."

I increasingly realise there are things I've picked up along the way, thanks to a very atypical path over the past 40 years, that could well be useful for others.

The goal of this book is thus not to try to teach you how to be a journalist, but to give you a little extra ammunition that may make the difference when the heat is on. My background in media is quite varied, so often in the coming pages, you may find me heading off on tangents. They were "lessons of life" that I can now pass on to you... for you to build on.

As Richard Yonge, best man at my wedding – boss of Riviera Radio in the early years (and someone whose opinion I have always treasured) regularly said, *"Keep it tight'n'bright, mate!"*... Yup. That's it in the end. In the coming pages, hopefully we will guide you as to the ways of doing that.

Photo credits - David Niviere, Markus Winkler

WHAT'S NEWS?

In a mass of information "noise" out there, the job of the journalist is to sort through this and find what might be of particular interest to the audience. It can be defined as "newly received or noteworthy information, especially about recent events". News value or newsworthiness has to do with how pertinent and current one particular story is in relation to other stories, specifically with regard to your audience. Taking this to the Nth degree, I call it *information intelligence*.

Finding news is of course the core of our business, and in the commercial world, a product launch or press release will often be a no-brainer when it comes to understanding what the story is about. If you are working in a competitive environment, with other radio / TV stations or publications in the same sector covering the same news, it is important to find an angle that makes your story better than theirs.

But what is better? And how can you achieve it?

Be first: This has always been very important in radio news, and is today important online. But the race to be first can come at the price of accuracy. Depending on your deadlines, and whether you have a strong online presence or not, the speed of getting the story out can thus be a key factor. In radio, news happens on the hour or half hour, and beating your competitor with a story in a key bulletin (i.e. 7 a.m.) can be extremely important. In the case of a trade show daily, we needed to be sure that all major news from each day of the show was published the next day at the latest – not the day after. For newspapers, deadlines used to be daily. Now stories also run in real time online, and being first – even by half an hour, can make a big difference.

Find the right angle: All stories have multiple angles and ways of being told. It is up to you to decide which, for your listeners, viewers or readers, is the most pertinent angle, via the way you present the facts.

Uncover information the others don't have: If you attend a press conference, make a point of asking for a separate interview or interviews at the end of the official presentation and Q&A (if possible). Keep your "smart" questions for the interview – not question time. It may even be the case that you will get your lead from the interview, which will give you a completely different and more interesting story than any of the others. Even if you DON'T have strong competition, do this anyway. You owe it to your audience to get the best story for them, and it often requires going the extra mile.

Look deeper: As already mentioned, press releases often come across our desks with the lead buried way down towards the end. Look for the story. Look for what is NEWS. The case may arise where you are given a press release to work on from a client – in order to turn it into advertorial (paid editorial content, labelled as such), and you can't find anything very interesting in there. Go digging deeper. A case at hand was when we were producing this kind of advertorial material for the official tourism marketing organisation of a very large nation at a very big trade fair. We needed to produce a number of pages of advertorial for each daily edition, based on the sub-exhibitors that were at their stand. For this, the latter were asked to send us press material, which we passed on to our journalists to write up into articles.

Much of the information received was in the form of destination "brochures" with very little news value, or was written with the general public as the target. One press release from a regional destination started out by telling us that this place had wonderful white sand beaches, swaying palm trees, and blue clear water. The journalist tasked with the story wrote it up pretty much along those lines. When I pulled the story, making the point that this was not news, the journalist told me that's all he had to go with, and that he'd done the best job he could with what he was given. I asked whether he'd done any extra research online, further to what they'd sent us, to see if there was any news there. He explained that he thought we should go with the "official" information given to us by the local tourism authorities, as that's what they wanted to put forward.

Here, we have to understand that a well-meaning tourism officer, who may be highly competent in welcoming travellers to a destination probably will not have had any media training, and he or she may not understand how best to put his or her destination in the best light for a tourism professional reading a show daily. Within ten minutes searching news about this particular destination, we discovered that a major airline had just launched new flights from a state capital to this place. THIS was a very good lead in a tourism publication targeting travel agents and tour operators. The fact the place had lovely beaches and swaying palms is nice, but most travel professionals probably already knew that. This was "news".

Different Ways Of Looking At The Same Event

For any "news event", a number of different stories can be told, depending upon your target audience. Take the case of a house fire. One radio news report might lead with the terrible traffic jam all over the eastern part of the city caused by roads blocked by the fire brigade. Another might tell the heart-wrenching story of the handicapped woman who was smoking in bed and was unable to escape the flames when fire broke out.

Another might lead with the fact that this was the third fire of its kind in the same estate. All are valid stories, and all can be good leads, depending who you are targeting.

Judging the weight of one story against another is done by putting yourself in the place of the reader, listener or viewer and asking yourself how important the story is to them. If it directly affects them in some way, it is more important than a story that may be "spectacular" but has no direct relevance to the person.

Another example was given by newsman Dan Rather, who, in January 2019, posted on his Facebook feed:

"Gotta love it. My daughter reports from Houston that the three lead news stories on a local radio station (97.1) this morning were, in order: A 'bobcat alert,' bobcat on the loose in a neighborhood; a wedding in a 'Whataburger' (so far as can be determined that's a world first) and-- number 3, the Rockets NBA team has defeated the woebegone NY Knicks. The cable news channels and big-time newspapers are focused on Washington and Venezuela, but in a lot of the country news judgements differ. When a prowling bobcat in the suburbs trumps Trump, who's to say the newshawks in Texas are wrong with their bobcat lead?"

News That Has A Palpable Outcome

One story, or series of stories, that I worked on in 1984, is a particularly good example of the way different kinds of news can be surprisingly interesting or applicable, and that it can be useful to sometimes sit back and question our judgement on news choices. Here again, I am going to talk about a situation in radio news, but don't forget that the concepts are the same, no matter what kind of journalism you are into.

Having worked in radio news in Sydney for a few years, in 1984 – at the age of 24 – I took on a new challenge. I was employed to create a newsroom for a regional radio station –

2LM Lismore. At the time, they had no newsroom at all, as the station belonged to the Northern Star newspaper group, and the on-air presenters would simply read the news from the newspaper. Not good. Of course, the advantage of radio news is its immediacy and the possibility to have interview "bites" and other audio inserts, and here, they were reporting only what had happened on the previous day(s). On top of that, newspapers are written for the eye, and radio news is written for the ear. So, with the morning talk show host, Ian Richards, who also happened to have some journalistic skills, we created a two-man newsroom, and yes, as I mentioned in the intro, we won the Pater award for best regional news presentation in the first year of operation – in 1984. But what made me even more chuffed with what we'd achieved in that first year was that we were also finalists in the "Best Single Event" news coverage – of any station in Australasia. We didn't win, but we made it to the top five. As it turned out, a Sydney-based radio station won the award for their coverage of a bank robbery and car chase through the streets of the city, all followed live on air. It was no doubt particularly spectacular, and must have made for riveting listening. But to me, our story – even though we were a two-man team in a regional station – was more important. It had a real, concrete effect on people.

It all started as my father and I were driving through Lismore just a few weeks after I'd started working there. A young lady was hitch-hiking, looking rather down on her luck, so we picked her up, and she told us her story. Her name was Jillian Hayden.

"I've been actively seeking a job, and I have been trying to develop my skills at the same time by going to college," she said. *"There's been a gross misinterpretation of our situation. I've been advised my appeal could take anything up to a couple of months, and during that time I am destitute."*

It's not often that radio new *directly* affects people. News can influence attitudes or tear at your heart strings, but how often is there a tangible result from the coverage of an event?

Jillian agreed to be interviewed, and this became the beginning of an incredible saga involving not just one, but dozens of young people in our region, and many more elsewhere. They had all been withdrawn from unemployment benefits. They were left in a situation where they couldn't apply for tertiary assistance, because they were only part-timers, they couldn't get unemployment benefits, because they were at college, and they couldn't find work. It was a case of a group of young Australians trying to better themselves so they could enter the workforce, running into locked doors all the way. The coverage was a long process. An exhaustive number of interviews were conducted to cover the situation as it progressed. This coverage had some marked effects. Jillian Hayden was placed back on unemployment benefits not long after our first story. The department had "forgotten" to tell her she was eligible for interim benefits in a case of hardship.

But then came the other students. Student James Bresnahan was told by a department officer that because he wasn't a "media megastar", he could basically take a jump. So, we interviewed him... *"All they seem to be doing for me is giving me a longer and longer run-around, and I'm meant to just exist on no moneys at all. I find it very frustrating and of course it allows me no time to continue my education... and it's really putting a hole in what I am trying to do to become employed."*

He continued: *"Social security aren't even telling people their main rights. There are several sections that are very relevant to our case."*

The day after this interview was aired on 2LM News, James Bresnahan was reinstated on unemployment benefits. It was as though the social security department's local operatives had figured that by placating the noisy ones, the rest would keep quiet. But WE wouldn't. It was too late.

In the next steps, through our lobbying, the plight of the

Northern Rivers college students was brought up in Federal Parliament. Shadow Social Security Minister, Senator Peter Baume raised the matter during question time in the Senate, addressing the question to the minister concerned, Senator Susan Ryan. Not only that, the matter was also raised in the Lower House by local member, Charles Blunt, who also attacked the government over its handling of the issue, citing our news reports as his source of information.

A major breakthrough came when, thanks to a good friend with connections at very high levels, we were leaked a copy of the very letter that had been sent to the regional department heads, telling them to crack down on these students: a letter which, at the outset, we had heard about, but the existence of which was denied by the regional director of social security.

We called back the same director we had originally spoken to – this time, live on air. When we read the letter to him – verbatim, I imagine he probably turned a very bright shade of reddish purple. It's a shame we didn't have the image. He sputtered and mumbled and hung up.

Not long later, Social Security Minister Don Grimes returned from an overseas trip, and told our news service he would "speak to" the state director about the problem. The result was that all part-time students were placed back on full-time benefits. As a result of our news coverage, laws were changed so this situation could not be reproduced, and the author of the letter calling for a crack-down on part time students – a planning chief for the department – was removed. The students won the day... because we enabled their voices to be heard.

This was news that had a real bearing on people, and even for listeners who themselves were not on the dole, the story had a direct bearing, as everyone knows someone who at one time or another has been in a tough situation.

While not every story will turn out to have impact like this one, it is your job as a journalist to visualise your audience, and write for them taking into account their level of sophistication in the topic, and what key points will interest them the most in the story.

The biblical approach

When it comes to looking for news, "Ask, and it shall be given you; seek, and ye shall find; knock, and it shall be opened unto you." Sounds obvious, doesn't it? And yet strangely many so-called news people today expect the news to fall into their hands. It's easy if you have a bunch of press releases to sub them and run them as though they are news. But press releases, even when they appear interesting, instantly place you in the same boat as everyone else running the story the way the PR company or government agent intended, and thus mean that what you are doing is not news, but just regurgitating something to which everyone else already has access. The remedy to this is to go looking for a better (or another) story.

I must plead guilty as many editors do of falling into the trap of occasionally using press releases as general fodder upon which the other good stuff is piled, resulting in a mix that is still palatable, interesting and useful for the audience. It greatly depends on one's time constraints and human resources.

On the wire

In my old radio days in Australia, we received reams of news from the "wire service" (in our case, Australian Associated Press – or AAP) in a seemingly never-ending pile of paper under the printer, and much of it could have been used as it was. But we always rewrote it to make it more "radio friendly" and also not to sound like the other guys down the road. When I say radio friendly, that means putting it into "spoken" language rather than a more "written" style. It meant finding simpler words and making sentences sound as though they were being TOLD to you, NOT read.

News services that had fewer resources and thus took the news directly from the wire were disparagingly pointed at as being "rip & read", as the newsreaders would rip the news off the wire and present it as it was. Given that AAP was a good basic supplier of news, this was not necessarily a bad thing in terms of correctness of information, it just meant your news service added no value of any kind.

Looking for news

So just where does news come from when it's not force fed to you from a wire service or through press releases? This depends very much on what kind of news you are working on, but the basic, clear and simple answer to this is "through methodical, regular contacts with all those in important positions in your field of interest, and through the development of trust with these people". In radio newsrooms, we followed all possible sources simultaneously, or at least as much as we could. We had emergency service radio frequency scanners to eavesdrop on fire brigade and police two-way communications. In some places, the fire brigade also had an information dissemination service linked to newsrooms, with which they could instantly send a voice message in the case of a major fire or catastrophic event; every morning in Sydney, and other state capitals, the police would give a daily early morning press conference on all the major crimes and important happenings over the past 24 hours. Journalists would also be allotted to "do the rounds" – calling a long list of numbers of different services that might have news of some kind. When I started the newsroom in Lismore, I created my own list of rounds for each morning – of police and other emergency services in all the surrounding towns. It wasn't long before we got on well, and as they realised I was not a gutter journalist digging up the dregs of the news, they were very happy to give me real information. They knew I would present it in the right way, and thus in some cases we even became friends and would occasionally "hang out". In Sydney, if the scanner alerted us to a major accident, a murder, or some other newsworthy incident, we would of course send someone out as fast as possible. Sometimes we would get there at the same time as the emergency services themselves; and occasionally that could get a bit dodgy. I remember almost running over a murder weapon (a shotgun) with my car on a rooftop carpark in Seven Hills. Another time, at 2UE, I was sent to an accident at Chatswood train station – a woman under a train. I arrived at three minutes to the hour. They said, "You're going live", and as they crossed to me, the train was backing off the remains of the woman, so I described the scene as I saw it, and most particularly, the fact that this inconsiderate act by this woman was causing havoc on the local transport system. People don't know that when they throw themselves in front of a train, it will cause hours of delays for tens of thousands of people as investigations are carried out and so on. We became hardened to this kind of thing, and seeing bodies didn't faze me after a while. Our desk editors were quite jovial about all that stuff.

Yucky stuff. Don't read the next part if you are squeamish...

"It's just a 'jumpee'!", one desk editor would puff and say in the 2WS news room, meaning this was someone who had committed suicide by jumping off a building, cliff or other high-enough object. We in fact didn't report on suicides. If we were sent to a "deadie" and discovered they were a "jumpee" (or other suicide victim), we would head straight back to camp. That's part of a journalism etiquette that we followed that said that if you report on suicides, for some strange reason it tends to encourage other suicides. It's also not interesting unless the event creates a massive traffic jam or stops the trains for hours. So, we avoided it.

By the same token, if a murder was just a simple "Man gets jealous and shoots wife", we would also head back to the station, unless it was particularly interesting in some other way. If it was a mass shooting, or a multiple deadie gory accident, THAT was good stuff for the news. People used to say, "Oh it must be hard covering that stuff". But you quickly become hardened to it. What did bug me however was not the occasional bodies. They were dead and gone. But someone screaming in pain, in a car smash somewhere south of the town of Casino in northern New South Wales... legs stuck under the dashboard as they cut-off the roof and extract his dead mates... that could be awful. Especially when you learn afterwards that it was he who stole the (extremely fast) car, outrunning the cops between two coastal towns, and losing control as he overtook a truck on a long curve – meeting another police car head-on, around 6am. He rolled, hit a tree roof-first, killing all three of his passengers. And he was left conscious to watch... and experience it all... in agony. I don't know if that guy survived in the end. If he did, he had some pretty heavy baggage to carry around for the rest of his life. In something like that, it may have been better to have been one of the passengers. The suffering probably didn't go on too long for them.

Then there was the guy whose physically handicapped wife was burned to death as she was smoking in bed in a small house in Sydney's inner suburbs. She fell asleep, the bed caught fire, and she couldn't escape. Her husband arrived and pushed past the police lines and SAW what was left of her on what was left of a bed in their burned-out house. He screamed like I've never heard someone scream, and was no doubt mentally scarred for life. It was terrible. That's when being a general news reporter can be shitty. I have diverged, but I feel it's interesting to give some insights into what you might see or do if you become a general news journalist on the road.

Following court cases was another task of the general news journalist. This gives one a different insight into humanity, or whatever term can be used to describe some of the monsters that pass through the system. It must be understood that anyone who commits a horrendous crime will always blame his condition on someone else, and oft times, there is some substance to this. I guess the most intense case I saw was in 1982: the two young guys who were convicted of the diabolic, cold-blooded killing of the taxi driver Raymond Savage.

I was sent to the sentencing of 21-year-old Steven Elliot and 18-year-old Terry Mark Hitchins. They, and another younger guy, who ended-up committing suicide in jail, hijacked the taxi, killing Savage – the driver – stabbing him countless times, laughing as they jumped on his body to watch the blood ooze out. They then put the body in the boot and, as they said, "made a barbeque" of him – burning the cab. It turned out Hitchins had killed another taxi driver the year before. They did this for fun. I looked at Hitchins as Justice Slattery sentenced him to life imprisonment with no parole. He looked like the epitome of evil. Really. But his accomplice, also hit with a life sentence, was the embodiment of the "nice guy next door". These people had gone out that night with a clear plan: "We are going to go out and kill someone and have a lot of fun doing it". Strangely, Hitchin's mother was a cab driver. I think there was a lot more weird, strange psycho stuff going on there than I could possibly imagine.

The question then is how do you report on stuff like this for the mainstream media? This is when temperance becomes a factor. Okay, you hopefully won't have to cover a lot of events like this. But if you do, the important thing is to put yourself in the seat of the person listening to, watching, or reading your story. How much do people need, or want to know? In something like this, of course, it's advisable not to give all the details.

Indeed, we, as journalists have a big role to play when it comes to deciding what information to present and how to present it. In my case, I never received any pressure to stop reporting on a story. But I know journalists can be pressured – either internally or externally. I was happy that when one advertiser of

2LM Lismore asked my boss, Steve Robinson, for us to take the heat off when I was reporting on a case of alleged misconduct, otherwise he would pull his ad budget, Steve apparently said, "If you feel like that, pull your ad budget. I trust our news team to tell the right story the right way, and if you don't like it, tough luck."

I am sure that this kind of reaction is not always the case in some, or even most media today, but as mentioned earlier, you have a role to play in selecting news based on a number of strict criteria, and journalistic integrity should STILL be an essential element of your job.

The art of the beat-up (or never let the facts get in the way of a good story)

"Beating up" news, or creating a story when none is really there, is an art that has been developed over the years – especially in the gutter press.

As they say in that business, "Never let the facts get in the way of a good story". I saw this first hand when Sharon Stone was in Monaco, invited by Prince Albert to play on his baseball team in a pro-celebrity match (where – as I explain in another part of this book how I managed to get a great interview with her). Sharon attended a few different events in Monaco, always accompanied by her then boyfriend – a very attractive guy a few years younger than her. They seemed to be quite a "thing". At the end of the baseball game, each team had a group photo taken by a small swathe of photographers present for the event. The prince was of course at the centre of the group, and Sharon stood at his side. As is the case for most team photos, each had his or her arm over his or her neighbour's shoulder. A day or so later, one of France's downmarket "people" magazines ran a huge feature on the fledgling love affair between Prince Albert and Sharon Stone. They had very skilfully taken the group photo and cut everyone else out except the unsuspecting, non-existent "couple"! With his arm around Sharon's shoulder, it did look as though they were close. But I had been there, and knew it was really fake news. The entire story – a whole page – was full of details of stuff that never happened.

But that's not the only place you will find beat-ups. I often get the feeling that when a journalist has been told by his or her editor to "do a story on X", that oft times the journalist – either through a genuine lack of material or through insufficient research – "invents" an article.

In May 2020, as Covid-19 topped headlines every day, a big news agency ran what I could only describe as a classic beat-up. On May 21, the headline read:

"France's coronavirus deaths on the rise again, at 28,132".

The story was running ten days after France had opened up – to a certain extent – after its first two-month lockdown. It began:

"French health authorities reported 110 new coronavirus deaths on Wednesday, an increase of 0.4%, bringing the total to 28,132, the fourth-highest in the world behind the U.S., Britain and Italy. The number of confirmed cases increased by 418 to 143,845, an increase of 0.3%, in line with the average rise per day seen since the unwinding of a national lockdown on May 11."

As we go down through the paragraphs, we then find this:

"The number of people in intensive care with COVID-19 declined by 5.3% to 1,794. The number of people in hospitals with the disease fell to 17,941 from 18,468 on Tuesday. Both numbers - key indicators of the French health system's ability to cope with the epidemic - have been on a downtrend for at least five weeks and peaked at more than 7,000 and 32,000 respectively in early to mid-April."

OK. So, let's try to figure out what the report is trying to state. For a start, a headline that says "deaths are on the rise again", to me means there is a new spike, or at least a sharp new rise in deaths. Something one should be concerned or alarmed about. But reading the article, this is not the case at all. In fact, May 17th had in fact seen 483, followed on the 18th by a correction, showing up as a negative figure on the chart, and the story pertains to the 20th.

The overall trend since the unwinding of the lockdown was in fact for fewer and fewer deaths per day. Each day, figures would rise and fall, but one had to look at the general trend, not a daily figure which could very well be influenced by a number of external factors. Further on in the story, we learn that not only is there no spike in the number of deaths, but that everything else continued on a nice downtrend. The story leads with the fact that this rise in fatalities now places France in the number four position behind the US, Britain and Italy. In that respect, France's position had been very close to that of Spain, and that had not changed. So that's not news.

I could almost hear the editor yelling out to a journalist: "Hey Ben, we haven't run anything on Covid-19 in France for a while. I want something on my desk by five o'clock."

In the end, what the story is really saying is "France continues on its path to recovery from the Covid-19 shutdown... much as it has for the past days" ... In other words, not a news story at all.

If the journalist wanted to run a story on how Covid-19 was affecting France, I am quite sure that with a little research they could have found some interesting angles.

One way to make this into a real story could have been to interview France's Minister for Health, at which time the minister could, for example, underline the fact that he was confident France was on the right track, and that ten days after partially lifting the lockdown, it appeared that the country was on the path to recovery, albeit that one would have to be cautious over coming weeks and months. The headline could read something like: "French government says nation is on track to Covid-19 recovery".

HOW TO WRITE:
THE BASICS

The most important thing to remember when writing is the "three Cs" – be **clear, concise** and **correct**. All news is written in what is known as the "inverted pyramid" method, meaning the biggest, heaviest, most meaty facts are at the top, and the details thin out as one goes down through the lines.

The visualisation of this structure leads a number of inexperienced writers to believe that they should put ALL the important facts in the first paragraph. This of course is not true. Good news structure does not simply follow the inverted pyramid principle, at least not in the first three to four paragraphs.

Language should always be simple and concise, and sentences must be short. Generally, 50 words is a maximum for any sentence in a news article. You will often find that a sentence longer than this will be so due to having several subjects. This means the very long sentence can be turned into several shorter ones, which will be far easier to comprehend.

The first paragraph – the "lead"

After the headline, the first paragraph sets the tone of the whole story, and encourages the reader to delve further into the facts provided underneath.

The first paragraph of an article is "make or break". It must be very short – no more than around 25 words, and say what the story is all about in very simple language. Avoid the trap offered by many press releases that include several facts in the first paragraph. PR writers do this on purpose in order to get their client's name, what they do, who they're associated with, and why they are doing it... all in one hit. They do this because they are asked to do so by their clients. It just doesn't work.

In order to engage the reader, it is essential to find the "news in the news", and run it as the lead. This might sound very obvious, but quite often, even highly qualified freelancers working for our publications manage to deliver stories where the lead is still hidden in the third, fourth, or even last paragraph. What is the newest, or most impactful and significant part of the story?

The second paragraph – "the pillar"

No, it's not simply a continuation of the first paragraph. In general (with some exceptions) this paragraph or sentence serves a very different purpose. It is the pillar of support – a kind of foundation. Its purpose is to give some background – sometimes going back in time – that allows the reader (or listener) who may not have been following the story until this moment, to grasp what it is all about. It is a kind of parenthesis before continuing on with the structure of the main story.

For example, if your news is about a union spokesman making an important statement concerning current strike action, it may go something like this:

France's waterside workers union has voted to continue strike action that has been severely affecting Marseille's docks over the past weeks.

Workers walked out on labour day after talks broke down

between the unions and management over ongoing pay claims. In an ambit log of claims, workers are seeking an eight percent pay rise, but management say their offer of four percent is already very generous, and they refuse to go any higher. The strike is affecting freight deliveries throughout the region as well as causing major delays to ferry services.

(Then, here, you can go into the news from the meeting, explaining the whys and wherefores of why they won't go back to work)

Note how the second paragraph goes back in time to explain to the listener or reader where the story is coming from. Remember not all your audience has been following each story religiously, so it is essential to place your story in its context. Even those who have been following the story may appreciate having a reminder of what it's all about.

The following paragraphs

The story must be pertinent and punchy from start to finish, with details, explanations and quotes; running smoothly and seamlessly. A rule of thumb to see if you have covered everything that needs to be covered is to throw the "five W's" test at it (who, what, when, where and why), not forgetting, in addition to this, HOW (often left out, no doubt as it doesn't begin with a W).

The last paragraph – the "kicker"

The last part should, when possible, leave one with an interesting thought or fact. It needs to work as a conclusion, wrapping up the story neatly and elegantly.

In the case of the union story, we might end with something like:

The union and management are due to meet in Marseille again tomorrow morning, however union leaders say they are not confident of an early end to the dispute.

In lighter stories, of course the kicker can be something funny or amusing. In any case, it should round off your story, and not leave it "up in the air".

Writing and rewriting

If you are writing a long feature, it is always important to go back over it a couple of times to "thin it down".

What peeves me today is when I see young, budding journalists, or even older ones, handing in copy that over and over requires the same corrections that had been made to the previous pages handed in by the same person. In the "Remington era" – an epoch when everything was typed, and desk editors marked the copy up with a heavy ballpoint or felt pen – you instantly saw where you'd gone wrong and the lesson sunk in every time you looked at the page.

In his wonderful book, "On Writing: a Memoir of the Craft", Stephen King tells much of his life story. And he talks about the time he landed his first job writing for a sports column in a local rag. His first articles had been "torn to shreds" (metaphorically) by his editor, John Gould, who then had said to him, *"Do I have to explain any of these marks?"*, to which King replied, *"No."*

Gould went on, *"When you write a story, you're telling yourself the story. When you rewrite, your main job is taking out all the things that are not the story."*

"Write with the door closed", Gould also told King. *"Rewrite with the door open. Your stuff starts out being just for you, in other words, but then it goes out. Once you know what the story is and get it right — as right as you can, anyway — it belongs to anyone who wants to read it, or criticise it."*

By the way, King's book is a great read (or listen – as he also made it as an audio book – read by the author himself). I heartily recommend it!

Objectivity

It is important to retain a degree of scepticism at all times. Beware of exaggerations – especially in press releases. Remember that what YOU write as a statement is a fact as you are concerned. This puts the onus on you and your news organisation to have checked the facts and be sure of what you're saying. The same goes for shining adjectives or claims.

"The government has announced a breakthrough in tackling inner-city crime" might be written in an official statement. But it is THEM telling YOU that there has been a breakthrough, perhaps arranging a mass of statistics to cunningly give that impression. So, pin the assertion on the government: *"The government claims it has made a breakthrough..."*

You should be even more rigorous with claims about technical, medical or scientific advances. Always check the facts. In the case of commercial news, such as what we run in show dailies, companies will often claim they, or their product are "number one worldwide", according to one or other research organisation. It's up to you to check the facts – either by looking for official lists by the research organisation, or by contacting them directly. If the organisation confirms the company is the "number one manufacturer of ..." worldwide, then we can in fact say that according to the figures of this research organisation, they are number one. Until then, we can only say, *"Company X, which claims to be number one worldwide..."*

The role of the media must always be to remain neutral, even though, in more recent times, many "big name" media have been polluted and influenced by the big bucks. I'll talk more about that later.

When it comes to reporting on government corruption and other misdemeanours, the veteran US news-man Dan Rather put it very well: *"The press is an essential part of how a government of, by and for the people is supposed to work. The people have a right to know what is being done in their name. And when the press finds that something is not right, we have an obligation to call attention to it."*

Dan Rather's creed is quite fitting in this sense. Here is an extract:

I believe in independent—fiercely independent when necessary— reporting. I do not believe in Viacom's version of go-along-to-get-along reporting, nor do I believe in reporting to serve the corporate interest at the expense of the public's interest.

I believe in news of value to the country, not in news simply for stockholder value.

I believe that a news network should not be operated just as an owner's asset.

I believe that a news network is a public trust. This I believe.

Well stated, Dan. After leaving CBS, Rather went on to work with Mark Cuban on HD Net, where he said he had total free-reign on his content.

NOTE: I strongly suggest listening to the audiobook version of Dan Rather's "Rather Outspoken – My Life in the News", which traces his life story as one of North America's most legendary newsmen. You can also follow Dan on Facebook, where his pertinent and timely posts have millions of followers.

Put plainly, it is our job to insist on reporting real facts, as we see or experience them.

The facts

Only in recent years have we learned that there may be such a thing as "alternate facts". This ludicrous suggestion was made by Donald Trump's press secretary not long after his election as President, when he had claimed to have had record crowds for his inauguration. This patently wasn't the case, but led to the concept that there could be two sets of facts – the ones the President was presenting, and the ones the mainstream media were reporting. Once we get over the idea that this wasn't a joke, it does bring us down to the very core of what we do. That is, reporting facts. It is up to YOU to decide which facts you should present, and in what order to present them, depending on a number of considerations. These include your demographic, your type of media, your time frame and how you want to angle your news/information with regard to your competition. But all that being true, the base of all you are presenting is facts – different, diverse facts. You absolutely need to check you have the correct facts – the "truth" in all aspects of your story. Making sure you get your facts right is also applicable when you are dealing with incoming press releases and other news that is handed to you on a silver platter. For anything that is strategic, find a way to check the facts. Don't be manipulated.

There are various ways of checking the facts, but in any case, even if you are working from a press release, it is important to double check what is being said. When facts quoted in a press release or in other base material may seem strange or false, you absolutely need to check them. Your second and third sources may confirm what seems to be strange or weird with regard to the story. If that is the case, just drop the part that bothers you.

Wikipedia is NOT a "sure fire" factual source

Consulting Wikipedia may be part of your fact-checking process. But remember, Wikipedia is simply a collaborative platform. It will often give you some good "rule of thumb" guidance, but it merely reproduces snippets from a broad range of publications – not all of which have faultless fact checking, and I have seen this on quite a few occasions.

Wikipedia relies on well-meaning contributors searching stable, reliable press sources to put together "articles" on different topics. But are they all well-meaning? I believe it is not totally impossible for a Wikipedia contributor who wants to put a "slant" on a story to make a "selection" of the more damaging articles about an event from which to construct a "story" on the platform, all within the rules of the game. The people reading the post will thus not have a totally balanced view of the subject.

Added to this is the fact that the actual organisers of an event cannot be used as a direct source of information. What? You heard me right. In the case of the World Music Awards, the list of prize-winners on Wikipedia was wrong, because the magazine from which it was sourced got it wrong. The event organisers sent me the official list and asked if it could be updated on Wikipedia. I updated it, and it was pulled down some time later, because the source was the organisers, not a magazine. So basically, if print media get a story wrong to start with, it will be wrong on Wikipedia. One of the sources of information in this case was simply an online blog in Miami. How these kinds of sources are "trusted" is beyond me.

Another Wikipedia alert happened when I was working for Renault Sport on the "junior formula" racing – Formula Renault 2.0. As I had virtually no knowledge about any of these (very young) drivers, I examined their blogs, Facebook pages, Twitter feeds and, yes, Wikipedia, to get information about them. Looking back, I should probably have gone personally to each team truck and asked them for an official resume of each of their drivers. But I didn't. In most cases, all was OK. Except one, where I met the parents of a driver who said, *"Oh, you're the guy that keeps saying our son is half Brazilian. He's not. He's all French."*

I happened to have my swathe of papers with me, including a print-out of the Wikipedia page about the driver, which stated in no uncertain terms that he was half French, half Brazilian. *"Oh, that,"* they said. *"Yes, we have been trying to get that changed for ages. But because we are family, we can't. It's crazy."*

To be clear, I occasionally use Wikipedia, and I believe it

serves a purpose. It is important, but it is certainly not without flaws or imperfections. Do not count on the information therein as being solid facts.

Encyclopaedia Britannica still exists, and has a solid process for fact-checking. Their adage: *"Editorial quality has been Encyclopaedia Britannica's top priority since the company was founded in 1768. Britannica's methods for ensuring quality have changed over time, but their purpose has remained constant: to generate and validate content that represents the best, most up-to-date knowledge available."*

The most obvious source is often simply the organisation or person being cited.

When in doubt, leave it out

In our day-to-day work, it is not unusual to spot a bit of information, either in an interview or in a text that has been edited, that you don't fully understand. The first natural reaction, especially for a young journalist, is to avoid asking about the "sticking point", for fear of appearing to be naïve or stupid. Wrong. What is even worse is employing what you don't really understand in a text, in the belief that, "Well, the readers are from this sector, or market. THEY must understand." Again, wrong. If you don't understand, the reader or listener most likely will not either, and it is quite possible that it was a mistake. Worse than that, the remark you didn't understand but reproduced may have a negative or derogatory implication.

If you haven't fully understood the meaning of a sentence or phrase, you have two ways of solving the issue. First is to go back to the person or source and dig out what this means. The second is to simply take it out. If a statement sounds confused, or a sentence doesn't make sense, dump it. Your reader, viewer or listener will be much happier for it.

Your point of view

Here's an interesting thing about your point of view when writing or presenting news: you don't have one. If you do, you are not a journalist – you're a commentator. It began with the onset of far-right wing media giving a heavy sway against "anything on the left", with presenters or editors openly commenting on issues. As a counter-attack, now the left-wing media tend to do the same thing. People who deliver this type of commentary are simply not journalists, but are paid presenters working for an organisation that employs them in the understanding that they will "toe the line". It's a choice on their behalf to sell out to the big boys – for the money, but it doesn't have to be your choice.

I have always believed that if journalists honestly report the facts – given only the parameters of demographic of their audience, they contribute to the reputation of their media, and to their consequent success. Unless you are writing the kind of magazine piece or producing a video or audio report that requires a "personal" angle in its presentation – a kind of review – your opinion should never, at any time, creep into a report. And in that respect, a review should also be as even-handed and factual as possible. The audience doesn't care how you "feel" about something. They want the bare facts. You are not the star of the show; your STORY is the star – if it is put together in the right way.

The fact of being able to compile excellent, even-handed, well thought-out, concise, clear and logical articles or reports that are easy to assimilate and understand can eventually make you a "star" reporter. That's what you need to aim for – not being the star of the article – which in the end makes you look puffed-up and conceited. That's not for you.

WRITING FAST AND WELL - YES YOU CAN

Harking back to my first radio news days at 2CC in Canberra, one of the first things I learned (and which everyone quickly learns in radio news) is that radio journalists have to write things very quickly. If it's five minutes to the hour, and a major news event of some kind has just happened, you need to be able to write a four-sentence (around 30 seconds on air) story before the top of the hour, ready for the news. You don't have an extra minute or so to ponder over what style or structure you are going to use. As a famous sport person once suggested, you "just do it".

"Churning" news copy was not only applicable to last minute stories close to the top of the hour. In radio news, it was all the time, from the start of one's shift right up to the end. In a newsroom where you have to produce news every half hour, we would generally write at least three versions of each story. This was so that people who might be listening to the radio for over an hour, getting ready for work in the morning, would not hear the same news story repeated from one bulletin to the next. Some might argue that there is only one right way to write a story, or one angle that is applicable at any one time, but in fact there are always different ways to tell the same story, even with a similar angle, while still keeping it valid and current. Sometimes a radio story would have a short intro and a sound grab from a witness at the scene of the action – or "actuality" as we called it.

Other times, we might have a reporter at the scene, and again we would have a short intro throwing to his 30-second report. A third version might be all text read by our newsreader. A story that ran at 6 am would thus not be re-run until at least 7:30 am.

The news was of course typed (in BIG type) on A5 size pages, and placed on the make-up board in the order of reading for each bulletin. The make-up (or layout) board was a sloped board with several lines of timber slats upon which the pages could be placed neatly; the bottom row contained the pages – in the order that would be read in the next bulletin, and the others had the pages that were "standing by" for reuse. Once read, we would stamp each page with the time it was read, and would generally never read the same story more than three times (four if we were really strapped).

The concept of doing rewrites probably changes across cultures. I once had a heated discussion with a BBC World Service aficionado who argued that the BBC wrote each story "perfectly", so it couldn't be rewritten, and of course could be repeated verbatim from one hour to the next. I guess it's a case of horses for courses, but I think for the audience, variety can be nice.

My first months as a cadet radio journalist found me struggling with this concept of having to write a lot of news, and write it very fast. How could it be possible to write something well if there wasn't enough time to think about it? In the end, it is like everything, however: with practice, one improves over time.

The capacity to write quickly and well at the same time is not something limited to good radio news journalists. It is also an essential quality for a number of TV journalists, daily newspaper news journalists and also in the case of those working on trade show (print or online) dailies. At shows that we worked on when I was editor-in-chief at Cleverdis, such as IFA or ITB Berlin,

ITB Asia, ITB China, IFTM Paris, Vinexpo Bordeaux and Hong Kong etc., the daily magazines were on the one hand the official voice of the show organisers, and on the other, were essential decision-making tools for the trade visitors. They needed to cut through the noise of the show and get to the essential news and information. To do this, the news had to be fresh, pertinent, relevant, and always correct. But given the bulk of information to wade through, the number of press conferences to attend and interviews to do, journalists do not have the luxury of being able to spend three or four hours on a single page 600-word story.

Some – even highly professional journalists working for big-name media – find it hard, or even impossible to combine speed with creativity and accuracy. This is not because they are bad journalists, but because they have often never had to do that before. If they are feature writers, they generally have days, or even weeks, to do one story. And the result may be great: a work of art. At a trade show, however, journalists have to be multi-talented, write fast, and find the news in a story even when it occasionally appears at the outset that there isn't any. Becoming a journalist who can do this makes one a highly-prized "rare pearl".

HEADLINES

According to David Ogilvy, five times as many people read the headline as read the bold copy. Headlines thus generally have two main roles: to grab the reader's attention, and at the same time to tell him or her exactly what the story is about. I say generally, because occasionally, an enigmatic headline can be useful if a story is quirky and lends itself to it. If the story is pure news, then the headline should be hard-hitting and summarise the story. For feature articles, headlines can and should be more creative. They can also tease, flirt, and hint - while not always giving away the lead.

Headlines must be accurate: in fact, in implication, in spelling, and in grammar.

A current trend, which was spawned by the tabloids, is towards the use of "hammer" headlines: 1-3 words without a verb, often using a double-meaning or subtlety. Examples include "Megxile", "It's Paddy Pantsdown", "Queen Backs Brexit", "Beatle John Lennon Slain", "Diana is Dead". A more explicit subhead then explains the news

When talking about a company or organisation, it can be good to avoid using their name in the headline. For example, for a travel guide, "Hong Kong's newest rooftop foodie destination" attracts the attention and tells the story, creating a little intrigue, as in order to discover the name of the place, one is obliged to read on.

A "capital" idea: The first word in the head should be capitalised as should all proper nouns. Most headline words appear in lower-case letters. Do not capitalise every word. (Some publications do capitalise the first letter of every word; we used to, but don't any more)

Double-deck headlines

In cases when you have a double-deck headline, the second deck supports the first one, it does not say the same thing in a different way. Never repeat a key word from one deck to another.

"Funny" headlines or puns

Some headline writers tend to overuse puns and phrases from pop lyrics or comedy sketches, and editors frequently have to restrain their use (I plead guilty to having done so a few times in the past). This kind of thing sits even less easily in copy, where only UK-born readers over 55 can identify. Again, the danger is excluding readers.

Rules of thumb:

Select key words from the story;
Think of the most interesting ways to attract the reader;
Use simple but powerful language;
Use numbers or statistics to make a point (when you can);
Is it in good taste?
Is it offensive in any way?
Can anything be taken in the wrong way?
How can it be improved/shortened without sacrificing accuracy?
Does it communicate clearly/quickly?
Any confusion?
Any odd words, double meanings?
Is it accurate, true?
Use active, short, action verbs;
Use present tense to indicate past ("Biden wins presidency"),

past perfect for past tense, and future tense for coming events;

Avoid puns, except for stories that lend themselves to a more light-hearted intro;

Avoid repeating principal words from one deck to another;

Avoid clichés like the plague;

In headlines, use digits instead of words (i.e. "10 ways", not "ten ways");

Don't exaggerate; maintain neutrality;

Don't pad heads with unnecessary words;

Avoid using exclamation marks!

SEO and headlines

When writing online articles (using Wordpress or Drupal), the use of seductive, emotional or sensory power words, along with numbers, will move your article up in the search engines. A good resource to learn more about this (at time of writing) is https://rankmath.com/blog/power-words/.

IS QUALITY
IMPORTANT?

T he book "Zen and the Art of Motorcycle Maintenance" by Robert M. Pirsig most likely does not top the "to read" lists for young up and coming journalists today. But it should. Among other things, the book is primarily an inquiry into values – in particular the value of quality. It's main character, Phaedrus, a teacher of creative and technical writing at a small college, had become engrossed in the question of what defines good writing, and what in general defines "Quality".

When asked by a colleague, "Are you teaching quality?", he literally loses his mind trying to fathom what quality really is, and to cut a long story short, the book is an intricate study of the topic. Quality in what we do in media is also something that tends to drive me (and number of those around me) to derision, and has occasionally been a root cause of conflicts I have had with people in the business.

It seems that over time, the idea that we should strive for the absolute best quality in all we do is slipping into oblivion. When talking about quality, it should be seen as an overall concept, covering all parts of the work we do. That said, pedantism should be avoided. The key is to have a very high level of quality in all aspects of the work; not total perfection, which of course doesn't really exist.

It is possible to look at any newspaper or magazine article (or radio news story) today and find ways to make it better, both in structure and in language. But that's not the point. If the article puts forward its key angle in an interesting or clever way, is well written, says what it needs to say with an economy of words and retains the attention of the reader, it has done its job.

The eyes have it...

Visual supports in print media can be a subjective nightmare. When asking people to send photos to accompany their press release or an over-the-phone interview, more often than not, we encounter problems. As the communication world today revolves around the internet, and many photos are used solely for this medium, very often people will send material that is not suitable for printing. The general rule of thumb for a print photo is that it must be at least 300 dpi (dots per inch) across, of a *size equivalent to that which will be printed*. Some people will send a photo saying, "But it IS 300 dpi!", without taking into account that it is much smaller than the actual space that will be taken-up by the photo in the magazine (or other print support). If used as such, the photo will be horribly pixelated, giving a poor result for the publication and damaging the public image of the person or place in the photo.

As budgets get tighter, the use of dedicated specialist photographers has been reduced or nullified, meaning photos often have to be taken by the journalists themselves. In the case of corporate or other activities for which press releases are being produced, photos are sometimes taken by employees of the organisation at hand. With the latest generation of cameras, and even the latest generations of smartphones, the result can be quite acceptable. But a journalist should not believe that just because he has a camera in his hand, he is now a photographer. Like everything else in this business, it is essential to learn one's trade. So, if you want to be a roaming reporter, writing articles and taking photos at the same time, you need to learn the fundamentals of framing, depth of field, lens characteristics, and basic image processing using software such as Adobe Lightroom.

This concept of "learning the trade" *in all its facets,* is increasingly being forgotten or neglected. A few of years ago, I was at a major annual global press conference in Malta for the consumer electronics industry. At the conference, a roundtable was held, during which print journalists explained how their work was evolving over time. They explained that as the internet and online video were becoming important parts of the way their organisations communicate, their bosses were asking them to record their interviews on video in order to supplement their work. My hand went up and I asked what training they were given when it came to becoming video cameramen and editors along with being print journalists. The answer was *"None".* So, when did the concept of learning your job become irrelevant? Why do people believe that if you are making a video for people watching it via the means of the internet, the quality doesn't matter? I believe the answer is that this concept came about as video and photo bloggers flooded the internet with material of all standards and quality, and that this then became a kind of "norm". In other words, video for major TV channels needs to be of a high quality (even there, now this is now questionable), but for the internet, "anything goes", even if you are a professional journalist. Back in the days of low bandwidth, indeed, the quality of all video on the internet was bad, as it was highly pixelated. But as 5G and fibre networks have become the norm, and video quality over the internet has surpassed that of broadcast TV, the shoe is now on the other foot. The need for excellence is rising over time as the audience chooses what it sees as quality rather than just quantity of images and information. This means those guys who went out taking rough videos of their interviews will now have to learn their trade, get professional help, or lose their audience.

While people seek fresh sources of news, they don't want to be bombarded with irrelevant data. In the end, it will all come back to quality of information... quality in its content and excellence in its presentation. For this, tomorrow's journalist will need to learn more, understand the needs of his or her audience, and be prepared for numerous new challenges.

Consistency in delivery

Quality is not just about delivering a good story. It's about *consistently* delivering something good. Note that I didn't say "perfect". You need to strive simply for what you are doing to be of very good quality, ALL THE TIME. Strive for that. You may never reach it... and we ALL make mistakes. We all have bad days. We all have times when we deliver something that is under par. But the goal has to be for consistently just a little bit better overall than the others.

So why just a little bit? I was once told the story of a racehorse that used to regularly compete against a former stable-mate, who ran just as fast as he did... well almost. In each race, over ten races, this horse won, while the other was just a nose or a whisker behind. After ten races, there was not even a full length's difference in the end result. But in terms of winnings, the first horse had won more than ten times more than the second. The moral to the story is that you don't have to be ten times better than the others. You just need to strive to be a little bit better than them all the time – in every aspect.

Another good example of this was the Australian radio "legend", John Laws. I worked alongside him at 2UE in Sydney for a short time in 1982/83 when I was a young reporter there. Laws always at that time held the number one position as mid-morning presenter on any Sydney station, and there was a battle between 2GB and 2UE for the overall number one position in the market. Having the number one position made a huge difference in advertising revenue, as many big companies would run ads with the "winning" station and pull them off the number two station. This meant the difference between being #1 or #2 – even if not huge in terms of listeners, was worth many millions of dollars for the station. When they figured out that having or not having Laws would make the difference between being first or second overall, there was a kind of auction for him, orchestrated by his agent, which meant that he became, in the early 80's, one of the highest paid radio presenters in the world. He made millions, which in radio was unheard of. Just as an anecdote… being in the studio with Lawsie was a bit strange, because when you were in there, you could hardly hear him talk. He used – very effectively – what we call "close mike technique" – where you talk softly next to the microphone in such a way as to bring out the timbre of your voice. I learned that from him – a valuable lesson, as when the voice booms out of the radio you have the impression that it is emanating from a kind of God. It's like a person standing right next to you, talking to you – and just you – with a "golden voice".

Microphone technique is thus extremely important when you work in radio (or on audio podcasts for that matter). Very few people today master this very well at all. Was Laws ten times better than his competitors? No. He just had the edge. And that made him MUCH more valuable.

STYLE

In this chapter, I am not going to try to reinvent the wheel. As Isaac Newton said, if you stand on the shoulders of a giant, you can see further than the giant. This is highly applicable when talking about language, because it has ALL already been invented and explained. It is possible to find numerous guides on writing style, many of which are good, and none of which I could outdo in terms of breadth of ideas covered. I would recommend checking-out the BBC Academy and the Guardian's news writing guide by Peter Cole. You will find direct links to these free online resources in the bibliography. A lot of what is written here is inspired by these resources.

George Orwell's six elementary rules are a good start:

Never use a metaphor, simile or other figure of speech which you are used to seeing in print.
Never use a long word where a short one will do.
If it is possible to cut out a word, always cut it out.
Never use the passive where you can use the active.
Never use a foreign phrase, a scientific word or a jargon word if you can think of an everyday English equivalent.

Or according to Stephen King: *"One of the really bad things you can do to your writing is to dress up the vocabulary, looking for long words because you're maybe a little bit ashamed of your short ones. This is like dressing up a household pet in evening clothes. The pet is embarrassed and the person who committed this act of premeditated cuteness should be even more embarrassed."*

Another great piece of advice was given by William F. Strunk: *"Avoid the elaborate, the pretentious, the coy and the cute. Do not be tempted by a twenty-dollar word when there is a ten-center handy, ready and able."*

Step Back

It is generally difficult to detach oneself from one's own copy when reading it through, but it is important to master this. Put yourself in the place of someone who has little or no knowledge about the story until now.

There is always an issue over how much knowledge one should assume, particularly with a story of which today's may just be another episode (see also the previous section on story structure and the importance of the second line which gives some background the the story).

You can't always go all the way back to the beginning for the benefit of a reader recently arrived from another planet, but you can include sufficient information to ensure all people can easily follow what you're on about.

In the section on "failed" press releases, this is particularly the case with a story from a technology company which would appear to be in nother language for anyone except those working in that company.

Active not passive

Always prefer the active voice in news writing, and particularly in intros. In active voice, the subject of the sentence is the actor doing the action of the verb: i.e. *"The company's directors will meet next week"*. In passive voice, the subject of the sentence is the one on the receiving end of the action: i.e. *"A meeting will be held by the company's directors next week"*. Active voice can also make a weak sentence more emphatic and give it greater impact. There are some exceptions to this rule, such as this one:

Active: *A rhinoceros trampled Prince Charming at a safari park today.*

Passive: *Prince Charming was trampled by a rhinoceros at a safari park today.*

In this example, the focus of the story is Prince Charming, not the rhinoceros. You want the royal name at the beginning of the sentence because that is where it will have most impact.

Passive voices as a safety net

Governments, politicians and officials of all kinds love the passive voice, because individual actions are buried beneath a cloak of collective responsibility. They say *"Mistakes were made"* instead of *"We made mistakes"* - and use phrases such as *"in the circumstances it was considered"*, *"it will be recognised that"* and *"it was felt necessary that…"*

Used in this way, the passive takes the life out of the action and distances it from any identifiable source. When things go well, the minister, company chairman or football manager says: *"I decided on this course of action."* When the response is less positive, this becomes: *"It was thought to be the right thing to do at the time."*

Natural writing

According to the BBC Academy, it is more natural to write *"The committee park their cars in the field"* than *"The committee parks its cars"*, because the committee is being thought of as a single group of separate people. In this case, I believe the BBC is wrong. The correct sentence would be *"Members of the committee park their cars"*, as a committee can't park cars; its members can. The same goes for any institution or group of institutions.

It would be correct to write *"The committee has voted to ban cars from the field"*, because the committee in this case is being seen as a single body.

Consistency is key

It is incredibly easy to change from singular to plural within a sentence if you let your concentration lapse. *"The company has issued a profits warning which could have a serious impact on their shares",* or *"A team of scientists has arrived in Hong Kong, and they will start their investigations into the outbreak of smallpox tomorrow."*

In sport, in the UK, teams are always plural. *"England are expected to beat Andorra",* or *"Chelsea have extended their lead at the top of the Premiership."* In US English, teams are singular: *"Notre Dame has produced 96 All-Americans and 7 Heisman Trophy winners."*

Obviously if you are writing for an American publication or for American radio or TV, the style will be very different to that adopted in the UK and Europe. In this case, I suggest referring to the CBS News Style Guide or the Associated Press guide book.

On the continent, I have noted, particularly in Germany, that a number of journalists use American English. As we are in Europe, I feel it is much more apt to use UK English in all publications.

Danglers in writing

Sound nasty - and they're pretty commonplace. Merriam-Webster's dictionary gives this definition: *"To occur in a sentence without having a normally expected syntactic relation to the rest of the sentence."*

What does that mean? Well, see what you make of these sentences:

If found guilty, the Football Association could fine the Arsenal players.

After eating my lunch, the waiter engaged me in conversation.

When trying to log on, the system rejects my password.

Phrases at the beginning of a sentence need a noun or a pronoun and will cling to the first one that comes along. This can make your writing nonsensical.

Reported speech

This is otherwise known as indirect speech - and many find it confusing. A lot of people have never been taught reported speech and this is a pity because it can help you to be clearer and more concise.

Briefly, it involves taking what was actually said and reporting it – *"The judge said that..."* followed by what the judge said.

The difficulty is that if the "said" word ("claimed", "insisted") is in the past tense, as here, the verb in the reported speech must be changed.

So, in the fairy tale, what the wolf actually said was: *"I will huff and puff and blow the house down."* As direct speech, that's fine.

But if you want to incorporate this threat into a script, the verb in the direct speech cannot be a simple present tense.

Right: *"The wolf **said he would** huff and puff and blow the house down."*
Wrong: *"The wolf **said he will** huff and puff and blow the house down."*

The change to the verb is not needed, of course, if you are directly quoting what was said, as in *"The wolf said: 'I will huff and puff and blow the house down'."*

Stay positive even if the action is negative

News is more engaging if it describes something that is

happening, rather than something that is not. So rather than *"The government has decided not to introduce the planned tax increase on petrol and diesel this autumn"*, it is better to say *"The government has abandoned plans to raise fuel tax this autumn."*

Quotes – keep 'em tight & bright

Short, incisive, direct quotes change the pace of a story, add colour and character, illustrate facts, and give personal experience. The use of a quote can add a different tone of voice. Quotes can inject emotion or passion, or answer the questions *"What was it like?"*, *"How did you feel?"*, *"What are you going to do next?"*, or *"What actually happened?"* (see also the section on interviewing).

Sometimes a quote can provide precision, when the actual words used are crucial. On the other hand, quotes that are too long, particularly from local politicians or bureaucrats, can bring a story grinding to a halt. It is best to paraphrase speeches and reports to focus on the main points, and to make them shorter and more comprehensible. It is a vital skill, as is using resported speech (see above).

Officialise

Language used in letters from bank managers or council officers, or read from their notebooks by police officers giving evidence in court, should always be avoided. People do not *"proceed"*; they walk. Police do not *"apprehend"*; they stop or arrest or detain. *"At this point in time"* is now.

Adjectives

Veteran Daily Mail and Daily Mirror columnist Keith Waterhouse wrote an excellent book on journalistic writing called Newspaper Style. It was in fact an adaptation of the Mirror style book he had been commissioned to write. In it, he warns of the dangers of adjectives, thus *"Adjectives should not be allowed in newspapers unless they have something to say. An adjective should not raise questions in the reader's mind, it should answer them. Angry informs. Tall invites the question, 'How tall?'"*

This test should be applied to all adjectives used in journalistic writing. If they add relevantly to the information being provided, they can stay. If not, avoid them. Too many writers believe adjectives add colour and style. Vague or general ones add nothing. *"Use specific words (red and blue),"* says Waterhouse, *"not general ones (brightly coloured)."*

Jargon, abbreviations, acronyms and foreign phrases

As so rightly pointed out by the Guardian's Peter Cole, all of us who work in organisations, professions, specific industries or bureaucracies are surrounded by jargon. We may regard it as shorthand to speed communication because we share the understanding of what it means, but, whether intentional or not, it is a protective shield that excludes those not in the know.

That is the effect it has when used in our writing. Those in the know understand; the rest do not. Anything readers do not understand makes them feel left out to the point that they may well stop reading (or listening/watching).

Redundant words

As Orwell said, *"If it is possible to cut out a word, always cut it out"*.

In day-to-day speech, people often tend to use unnecessary extra words, such as *"I thought to myself"* (who else would be thinking in your head?), or *"As the old adage says"* (an adage is an old expression, not a new one). When writing news, it is important to cut to the bone.

Here's an example I heard on the radio recently:

"The fire, which completely destroyed the caravan, is thought at this stage to have been accidental."

This could have been said as follows:

"The fire, which destroyed the caravan, is thought to have been accidental."

If the caravan was destroyed, it was destroyed. Partially destroyed doesn't exist. That's called *"damaged"*. If we are talking about it now, that means we are *"at this stage"*. It is evident that if other news comes to light indicating the fire was not accidental, then there is a news update.

There are a number of other cases that are worth mentioning:

Very unique: i.e. *"Mark Knopfler has a very unique style"*. Something cannot be "very" unique. Unique means *"one of a kind"*. It thus either is or isn't unique.

Past experience: by definition, experience comes from the past. Past history is a similar booboo.

In five years' time: "time" is redundant. If we are talking years, we are talking time.

In my opinion: Well, if you are saying it, it is probably your opinion. If someone says it in an interview, cut out these spurious words. Same goes for "I think".

Estimated at about: You can't say *"estimated at exactly"*. It's either *"estimated at"*, or *"valued at around"*.

Exactly the same: the same.

Added bonus: bonus.

Absolutely essential: essential. Same goes for *"absolutely certain"*, or *"absolutely sure"*. If you are certain, you can't be *"partly certain"*. It would be like being partly dead or partly pregnant.

12 midnight or 12 mid-day: midnight or midday. Here again, there is another trap, as some people use "12 a.m." or "12 p.m.".

Neither one is correct... or, should I say, both are exactly the same. AM means "Ante Meridiem" – i.e., "before mid-day". PM means "Post Meridiem", i.e., after mid-day. Thus, 12 a.m. means 12 hours before mid-day – so obviously midnight. 12 p.m. means 12 hours after mid-day – so, again, it means midnight. As they say, "go figure". Prefer to simply use midnight and mid-day.

4 a.m. in the morning: This is actually a tautology. It is just 4 a.m., or 4 o'clock in the morning. Someone please tell Mike Oldfield. I guess in Moonlight Shadow, it just sounded good.

Word and phrase redundancy, when taken an extra step, fall into the category of tautology.

I could add many examples to this list. But I think you've got the point. That, by the way, is another one. "Got": one of the most spurious, useless words in the English language. "You have got a nice dog" could be shortened to "You have a nice dog". "What have you got there?": "What do you have there?" ... The list goes on. So I think you *have* the point.

Tautology

A tautology is saying the same thing twice (or more) in different ways in the same sentence. This is something we often find in pontificating politicians' speeches, as they desperately endeavour to pad a vague single thought out into something that sounds important. Typical examples of simple tautology include phrases like, "I, personally would disagree", or, as mentioned above, "At 6am in the morning". A great one we come across these days is "a new innovation". Unwittingly, journalists may fall into the trap of quoting this clap-trap verbatim, however it should be avoided.

In 1986, when running the newsroom at 2LM in Lismore, Australia, we started noting tautologies as we heard them in interviews or in our own or other stations' news, and we pinned them to what became the "Tautology Wall". It was only a few months before it was full. It was so hilarious that one of our young presenters compiled the "pearls" into a book that she shared around the station.

To this day, I can remember some of the best ones, like *"The flood water is now off the road, but it's still in the river"* (more just plain stupid than a tautology), or *"an armed man with a hand gun"* (it would be hard to find an unarmed man with a hand gun).

The very best was attributed to Charles Blunt, the Federal Member for Richmond, who, just elected, gave his maiden speech to parliament, a copy of which arrived across my desk. It began, *"Australians, I believe, are basically self-reliant, with a preference for looking after themselves, rather than being looked after, especially if the price of being looked after is a loss of freedom."*

Wow. A quadruple whammy tautology. It was the tautology to beat all tautologies. Still giggling, I called a friend at the Sydney Morning Herald, where they had a "funnies" column on the front page, called "Column 8", and repeated the phrase to her. It took some time for her to regain normal composure before assuring me that this would top the list the next day, which it did. About a week later, I attended a luncheon with Charles Blunt, where I told him I thought his maiden speech was interesting.

"Yes, but some bastard quoted me in Column 8", he grunted.

"Oh, was that the part where you said, 'Australians I believe are basically self-reliant (etc. etc.)?", I questioned.

"You bastard!", he said, having understood straight away who the culprit was. I wasn't too sure just how humorous his expletive was, but in any case, I had had my fun, and now had a strange tingling sense of power, as I began to understand the ability we, the media, had in terms of making or breaking someone. It was of course in his interest to say "you bastard" in a humorous way, as I ran the only radio newsroom in his

constituency. He was, as it turned out, a nice bloke.

Pedantism

Every journalist can generally pick holes in his fellow journalists' work without too much trouble. Remember we have time constraints, and often have to make quick decisions on style as we're going along. It is important to avoid trying to strive for perfection to the point of being pedantic, otherwise you will probably never meet your deadline.

That said, quality is essential (see the section on this). So, while a line must be drawn higher rather than lower, it should not be so high as to slow everything down to a standstill.

Numbers

It is not always necessary to use exact numbers. Rounding them off can make a story much easier to assimilate.

If a ministry of tourism sends you a pile of detailed statistics, it will be much more telling if you say *"Just under 30-million international tourists visited country X in 2020"*, than *"29,762,567 tourists visited country X in 2020"*. Or you might want to say *"around 30-million"*.

ALL IN CAPS? No thanks.

Quite often, in fact increasingly so these days, brand names in corporate press releases are written ALL IN CAPS.

An example: *"We are pleased to welcome PAUL GAUGUIN CRUISES to our PONANT family,"* noted *Jean-Emmanuel Sauvée, Founder and President of PONANT.*

Sorry guys, but Paul Gauguin was a person, and I'm sure he didn't spell his name all in caps. Please don't do him the disservice of YELLING his name, which is, in fact, what you are doing by putting the name all in caps. If you, as a journalist, receive a press release like this, you will have to weed through and change all the all-caps words back into normal words. It's not because some branding/marketing person has decided the company name will be written in caps on its letterhead or website (or in press releases), that we have to follow suit.

Thus, do your readers a service, and take out the yelling. The REASON of course that people put BRAND NAMES all in caps is that they STAND OUT better like that – and sell the brand.

Don't let yourself be manipulated by the marketing boys.

TV, VIDEO, RADIO & PODCASTS

B roadcast media, while having the same journalistic foundations as print media, have a whole different set of rules. They can be a good foundation for other kinds of journalism, and vice-versa.

The British literary critic Cyril Connolly once said: *"Literature is the art of writing something that will be read twice, journalism -- what will be read once".*

He might have added that radio journalism is something that cannot be read at all, and is generally heard only once. Clarity and accessibility are thus fundamentals. The reader of a book, newspaper or magazine can go over an obscure passage until it is clear. The listener to a radio or TV broadcast (or live streaming media online) can only be confused or annoyed – or both. Confusing radio (or TV) is just as bad as boring radio – it results in the listener turning off. An advantage with podcasts is that if someone doesn't hear something right the first time, they can go back over it at will.

Writing for live audio or visual media, you must say what you have to say in as simple and direct a way as possible, without compromising its essentials. The structure of the sentence should be plain, with familiar and colloquial words. Anything that is clumsily expressed, verbose, or imprecise will obscure meaning for those without the means to revisit what has been said.

When writing scripts for the spoken word, it is very important to put the words on paper as they would be said in normal conversation. The simpler the better. Write the way you talk... but that is easier said than done. Taking this to the "Nth degree", in the 1980's, in the newsroom at Radio Monte Carlo (broadcasting in French, and at the time one of the most listened-to stations in France), each journalist would "tell" or dictate his news story to a stenographer, who would type it exactly the way he was saying it. A bit extravagant perhaps, and I don't know if other French stations did that at the time, but nevertheless effective in ensuring the script was for the spoken word.

Never write sentences containing quotes, but use reported speech. For instance, you might write, *"Judge Smith told the jury to pay particular attention to the evidence that was given by the scientific brigade."*

You should NOT write, *"'I would ask that you pay particular attention to the evidence given by the scientific brigade', Judge Smith told the jury."*

Keep sentences very short. The listener or viewer only has one chance to pick-up and absorb what you have written.

Always use present tense (unless there is no other solution – then try to use past perfect tense).

Rather than say *"40 people were taken to hospital this morning after a train derailment in Oxfordshire"*, you can say *"40 people are being treated in hospital following a train derailment this morning in Oxfordshire."*

As they are still being treated, it's still current. If the train accident happened yesterday, and most of the people are now out of the hospital, you might have a new angle: *"Accident investigators are today being sent to the scene of a train accident in Oxfordshire, which yesterday left 40 people injured."*

... and so on.

Locations

When talking about a place, first mention the town or city before mentioning the street. When listening to someone talking, our mind pictures what they are talking about. So, if you say *"The attack took place in Nice, along the Promenade des Anglais"*, people will follow more easily than if you say, *"The attack took place on the Promenade des Anglais, in Nice"*. In the second example, the listener's brain doesn't connect to where the incident happened until it hears "Nice", because unless the person knows Nice, they may not have heard of the street name (albeit famous).

The same goes for such things as travel reports, when listing late or cancelled flights, or problems on the road. Say where the flight is going to or from before announcing details of flight number and times. Like that, someone listening to the radio who knows they have to pick up someone who is arriving from London Heathrow will instantly prick their ears up when they hear that first – i.e. *"We have a flight from London Heathrow arriving late this morning. It's flight BA123 due to arrive at 10am, and it should be arriving 30 minutes behind time – at 10:30"*.

For radio or TV, it's important to spell complicated words phonetically, to make them easier to read. If necessary, break them up with hyphens. In some newsrooms, proper nouns were written all in caps to make them stand out. This can be useful. Complicated numbers can also be written out like this: "Two-million-33-thousand-225". It's easier to read out loud than "2,033,225". However, as most people will simply not remember details such as this, it is in fact more useful to round up the number to "just over two million", or "around two million". In almost all cases, an exact number is not vital to the story. By the same token, be sparing with percentages. Almost a fifth is more accessible than 19 percent.

When writing for the spoken word, never split words from one line to the next (with a hyphen) or split a sentence from one page to another, as it makes them harder to read. Finish the last sentence at the bottom of the page or pass all of it to the next page. Lines should be double-spaced.

Short phrases, short sentences

For the spoken word, this rule is even more important than for the written word. Keep your sentences short and simple. One of the golden rules - used especially in news - is "One thought, one sentence". Do not clutter your sentences. Write in easy-to-say phrases. If there is more information, make other short, simple, easy-to-comprehend sentences from it. Do not jam one sentence or paragraph full of detail and ideas until the listener's mind spins. The listener will mentally switch off (if not physically). Allow one thought, fact or idea to follow another, to flow on.

Speaking style

Any good presenter will never sound as though he or she is reading. They should sound like they are telling you something... talking to you.

Read what you have written to yourself, and avoid sound clashes and groups of words that are difficult to say when strung together. The late British news reader Laurie MacMillan was once presented with a story which contained the words *"dismissed this as a myth"*. She pointed out rightfully that this was not fit to be broadcast. Test words to make sure they can be read aloud without causing problems. Test phrases to make sure they do not cause obstructions and that they flow from point to point. Eventually, you will "hear" your words as you write them.

When writing for the spoken word, do not use punctuation

that you cannot convey through expression or pauses. Remember that you can't read brackets or colons or any punctuation aloud. Use visual clues such as dashes and dots for pauses, and underlining for emphasis. Unlike what your teacher used to tell you, sentences can begin with "and" and "but". But not all the time.

In the layout of your script, identify all the components for the sake of easy and fluid production. In the case of throwing to an interview or other insert material, give clear cues for the beginning and the end of the bite. For example:

And the Prime Minister says the new legislation will be tabled in the next two weeks:

Audio 1: In: "I wish to make it clear that my policies…"
Out: "… until the next election."
Duration: 43 seconds

Now I'm looking, now I'm not

For video, if you are presenting to camera, avoid cutaway side-shots. This is a trend that has come about in past years which goes against all principles of communication. It drives me nuts.

So, why it so bad? A stand-up report – looking straight into the camera – is a way of talking directly to the person watching the screen. It's very personal: one on one. The person watching really feels you are talking to *them.* It's not just a TV presenter presenting; you're a friend telling them a story.

That ended when people started using cutaway shots to "add interest" to the edit – wherein someone with a hand-held camera or iPhone shoots from one side as you are talking to the main camera. It produces an effect of *"Now, I'm talking to you… now I'm not".*

People who do this in video editing have never learnt the

rule of communication that says you are a communicator, not a "presenter". Often, it will come from a video editor who thinks it looks "cool". While it's a trend or a fad, it is subliminally disconcerting for the viewer. Don't do it.

By all means, however, feel free to use cutaway shots during an interview, while you, the interviewer, are looking at the interviewee, not the camera. It is just a different angle to view two people talking in that case. You can start with a direct chat to the main camera, then turn to your interviewee, keeping your eyes on him or her from then on, and with the second (or third) camera doing cutaway shots, to augment the visual interest of the segment, which should, of course, also be augmented with other illustrative shots.

Using a prompter

Prompters used to be quite expensive purpose-built contraptions that hooked onto the front of the main camera you would be looking at, run by a trained operator.

Basically, it's a one-way mirror in front of the camera, or a glass panel placed in front of a lectern, on which the text scrolls at the same speed that the presenter is reading. A poor operator could make using a prompter quite hellish and scary.

If being used live, be very careful not to deviate from the script on screen. This can cause you – and the operator – to get lost, with what can be quite dire consequences. One time at the CES conference in Las Vegas, a major electronics company had a big-name film director on stage – using a prompter for his presentation. To start with, he seemed very nervous to be up on stage. He then started ad-libbing, and lost his place in the presentation. This caused him to freak-out and freeze up... following which he muttered *"I can't do this"*, and ran off the stage.

The prompter can be a great way of doing video that looks like you know the entire script by heart. And today, cheap solutions exist using a tablet as the "screen", and with highly sophisticated scrolling that follows the speaker exactly. When using a prompter, it is important not to remain static, but to regularly move your head just a little, or the viewer will be attracted to the movement of your eyes – the only thing that's moving. It can be quite disconcerting.

Do a couple of air checks (dry runs) using a prompter to find the best way to avoid this.

You have an audience of ONE

Indeed, when on radio or TV, it is extremely important not to imagine that you are talking to tens of thousands, or even millions of people, but to just one person.

Why is this? Because the person listening to the radio or watching the TV or a podcast video is generally alone, or, in the case of the evening news, is just a family or couple sitting and watching the TV.

The listener or viewer may be an elderly pensioner sitting quietly at home, a carpenter on a construction site, a truck driver on the open road, a student working on research at home, a hospital patient, or a parent at home looking after his or her children. You are communicating with each listener on a personal basis.

This is one of the very first things I learned in my radio career. A presenter who talks to his or her audience as though they are simply one person listening has the game won. When I hear people come on air and say, *"How are you all today?"* – I wonder, *"How am I all? Huh? I am all OK I guess."*

Radio and TV can and should be intimate media, where the listener feels like he or she is listening to a friend talking to them, not a presenter presenting. It may be a highly authoritative friend in the case of a news broadcast, but a friend nevertheless. I have also seen this technique used by keynote speakers. Have you ever had that feeling that they're just talking to YOU? This is what you should aim to achieve.

A radio presenter I knew in Monaco would place a stuffed plush monkey toy on top of the panel in front of him, and would talk to the monkey when on air. It had the desired result. A BBC staff training officer once put it this way: *"It is not your vocal mechanism, but your manner of speaking that determines your broadcasting value."*

Radio: theatre of the mind

When writing for radio, or, for that matter, for an audio podcast, remember the old adage that radio is the *"theatre of the mind"*. Through your words, you are not only telling a story, you can literally paint a picture in someone's head. Words convey images, emotions and atmospheres. In this way, through the creative use of your words, you can set your listener dreaming of the place or thing you are describing. Good radio writing is thus the art of converting the ideas of the writer's imagination into pictures in the listener's mind.

As Robert L. Hilliard wrote: *"Radio is not limited by what can be presented visually. The writer can develop a mind-picture which is bounded only be the extent of the audience's imagination."*

Unlimited forms of physical action can be conjured up in an instant, vast spaces crossed in a flash, scenery and sets constructed at once, characters take on physical form, storms break, volcanoes erupt, thousands cheer, dragons roar, the seas rage, locomotives hurtle, and so on, ad infinitum.

As an early, but fantastically successful example, of the power of radio's imagery, listen to Orson Welles' adaptation of H.G. Wells' "War of the Worlds". Attempts to do the same thing visually have failed. So much depended on the pictures conjured up by each listener's own fears and personal "chamber of horrors", given the lead by Orson Welles and his production team. It was in the writing that the effect was given a chance to be fulfilled.

To summarise, here's a useful list of rules for writing for radio and TV (from the Australian Film, Television and Radio School):

1: Write words in the way they're spoken;

2: Use abbreviated forms: i.e. won't, rather than will not;

3: Use short sentences;

4: Write conversational dialogue, not statements;

5: Use simple words, not long ones;

6: Use well known words, not little-known ones;

7: Indicate pauses by dots or dashes;

8: Underline for emphasis;

9: Avoid over-use of the letter "s" because of its sibilant sound;

10: Be careful of assonance - same vowel sound - and alliteration - same beginning letter;

11: Round-out large numbers - 488,978 becomes nearly half a million;

12: Use comparisons rather than measurement - not recommended is "six millimetres long and one millimetre across" - better is "as small as a pin";

13: Use repetition for emphasis and to create effect - "as deep as the deepest deep in the middle of the deepest sea";

14: Use punctuation which will assist the reader of the script;

15: When writing a talk, write it like you would write a letter to a close friend;

16: Make your words mean something - not very meaningful is the thought "there are quite a lot of fish in the sea";

17: Be careful of time references - "good morning listeners", "next week", "this month";

18: Do not use lists of things - lists are really bad on radio. They're difficult to read entertainingly and quite impossible to remember.

19: Write sentences in the simplest and most direct way;

20: Use descriptive words to add colour and meaning - but be careful not to over-use them;

21: To the listener, the programme is happening now - write it as if it is;

22: Try to reproduce the natural rhythm of speech in your script; Read your script aloud after drafting;

23: If writing the script for someone else, make notations on the script (preferably in capitals to differentiate them from the words themselves). You can show inflexion, indicate if you want the pace speeded up, and so on;

24: Type your script double spaced and with a clear margin on each side;

25: A typical news broadcast is read at a rate of around 140 words a minute. Get into the habit of timing what you write.

26: Remember radio is the theatre of the mind, so when you can, evoke images that can get the listener imagining what you want him or her to see in their mind.

INTERVIEWS

The inclusion of interviews in any medium can add flavour and interest to your story. A good interview can also be a quick and easy way of presenting information that in a number of cases can be productive and communicative. A poor one can be just the opposite. A good interview depends, of course, on the ability of the interviewee to get the information across in an interesting and efficient manner, but this will be highly dependent on the skill of the journalist in conducting the interview correctly.

The importance of putting your interviewee at ease

At the beginning of 1984, when I had just moved to Lismore, I had a girlfriend who had admitted to me that in her teen years she had been an alcoholic. She would grab a secret drink before going to school, and sneak swigs from a hidden hip flask during class. She said she did this because she was terribly stressed at the idea that a teacher may call her to the blackboard and ask her to talk in front of her fellow students. She thought she was the only one who was so stressed out at the thought of talking in public.

One time she came along with me when I was covering an outside event, where I was to interview a politician for radio. She said to me afterwards, *"He was shaking like a leaf when you were talking to him. Why? I thought I was the only one who got nervous like that."*

It turns out that even public figures can become nervous when being questioned in a public forum – even by a young radio journalist. As it turns out, in any discussion, it's the one who asks the questions who has the power. The one answering is forced to respond directly to what you have asked, and this being "put on the spot" is often very stressful for people, even when they are accustomed to being interviewed. The result can be that the interviewee might give pre-thought, set answers, or that he or she will head off on tangents without really telling you what you want to hear, as their brain struggles to put together their thoughts.

For this reason, it is essential to try as much as you can to put people at ease before entering into an interview, and keep them at ease during the interview, by lightening-up from time to time. One problem, in the case of TV and radio in particular, is the microphone pushed up under their nose, creating an instant barrier, and placing them in an unnatural situation that causes them to be on guard and less likely to be open and candid with answers.

To counter this, where possible use a lapel mike for TV and pin it to them well before the interview starts, in such a way that they forget they have it on. Talk to them about the weather, their families, sports… basically anything to get their minds off the fact they are being interviewed. Then, when you start the interview, begin with light-hearted comments to keep them at ease.

For print interviews, I try to place my recorder (currently a smartphone) on the table well before the interview starts – already in record mode – and break the ice with a few other questions before getting into the thick of the interview.

If you are in their office, feel free to flatter your interviewee on his or her taste in decorating – commenting on things you may like. But be genuine here; false flattery sounds false. However, if they have a painting you really like, or if they have an original item of clothing you find interesting, say so. Everyone likes being flattered on points of taste. On another tack, you may wish to ask them about their recent holidays.

The American media writer Robert L. Hilliard put it like this: *"An interviewer must be at ease, knowledgeable, vitally interested in the work of the person being interviewed, and professional in the conduct of the interview. Basically, an interview follows a question-answer format, with an introduction, a main segment or body of information, and a conclusion. In style of performance it must be natural, straight-forward and conversational."*

It is essential for the interviewer to have a clear purpose in mind, be well-informed on the subject, and be clear as to the interview's ultimate use.

The English interviewer Jack Pizzey once said, *"I tend to go into an interview knowing what a person has it in them to say. I regard myself as something of a midwife, making the birth as easy as possible."*

A sense of assurance and self-confidence in the interviewer thus should communicate itself to the interviewee, who may, as mentioned, be nervous about saying the "right thing".

But an interviewer can only be self-assured if he or she is fully prepared.

Organising an interview

The British military's "seven P's" are very applicable here: Proper planning and preparation prevents piss poor performance. This applies to the research required in order to conduct a great interview, but it also applies to the organisation of the interview itself.

As with other things in life, if you want to "conclude" with a fanfare, it is essential to get the preliminaries right. If you plan to interview anyone of any importance (that's generally why you will be interviewing them), find out first who you have to go through in order to organise the meeting.

Sometimes this may be simple; sometimes not. In some cases, you will be asked to send a set of questions beforehand. If you are asked to do this, by all means do so, but specify that you may ask some other questions as the conversation progresses.

If by serendipity you have a potential interviewee in front of you, and you are burning to do an interview, I recommend asking them politely whether they may be available, and if so, who you should talk to in order to organise this.

Most of the time, celebrities of all kinds have agents who look after their agendas, and they will need to be involved in the planning stage. If you are lucky and your celeb says, *"That's fine, I have a few minutes right now"*, of course go for it. But don't try to paint them into a corner and force them to do something on the spot just because they are there.

This advice flies in the face of that which would probably be given by many of my peers, but this, to me is the best way to go. In the end, the interviewee will feel more comfortable, will be more open, and will trust you much more thanks to your integrity in the planning stage.

A good example happened in the early 90's, in the form of an interview I managed to organise with American actress, Sharon Stone, when she was in Monaco.

As I was presenting the weekly TV magazine show, Sunday, on Télé Monte Carlo, the organisers of a celebrity baseball match had invited me to cover the event up on the hills above the Principality. Along with the likes of Prince Albert and Roger Moore, Sharon Stone was there for a bit of fun while she was in town. I asked Kate Powers, who had organised and was running the event, to introduce me to Sharon's agent, which she did. I explained that I had a show on the local TV station and that I would greatly appreciate a few minutes with Sharon for my report.

At the right moment, when the star was resting up between games, the agent explained to her that I was there waiting on the side-lines, if she could spare a moment. She came over and gave me a great interview which was the highlight of my show. As the interview was under way, a fellow journalist – who worked for People magazine – gravitated towards us, and as soon as my interview was done, he leapt-in and asked Sharon for a few words. She said no. She was sorry, but she was not available for another interview.

Think about it. People was probably the biggest selling magazine in the world, with maybe 50 times more audience than my show. But she said no. The People journalist I am talking about is a friend, and a top-line journalist. He may have organised something afterwards with her, but right there, unless you went through the right channels, it didn't matter who you were or for whom you were working. Good lesson.

Another, even more extreme example, came at the World Music Awards in 2001. One of my "other" activities since the mid 90's has been that of annual "head of media" for this huge event, which primarily took place in Monaco, but had also been held in Las Vegas, Hollywood and London. In 2001, having interviewed the French supermodel Laetitia Casta at the Hôtel de Paris in Monaco as part of a report for the BBC World Service, I suggested she could perhaps come back a couple of months later to the World Music Awards as a presenter, which she happily agreed to do; with planning carried out by her dad and her then PR agent, Jean-Paul, who accompanied her to the awards.

Laetitia was exceptionally nice in accepting to do a whole swathe of interviews on the day of the show – which we organised one after the other in a Riva boat in the Monaco harbour. She was adorable and wonderfully accommodating the entire time. Then, in the evening, just before the awards show, as I was escorting her along the red carpet, a (major) Italian TV crew jumped out in front of us, and started shooting questions at her. It was clear Laetitia was not keen on being "pushed around", so I told them it was not interview time, and that this was not the way things were done. But they insisted, with the kind of arrogance, brashness and rudeness some of these interviewers acquire over time. Again, I asked them to let us past, warning they would be kicked out if they kept on blocking the way, as they were not even supposed to be on the red carpet. They told me their channel was a major partner of the show, and that they could do whatever they wanted. I called over security and had them removed – not only from the red carpet – but from the entire event. Partner or not, you play by the rules; you are polite, professional and organised. John, the show organiser, told me they complained bitterly to him, and he told them he supported my decision. You don't boss people around, and you certainly don't boss supermodels or stars around – even if you're from a big TV network. The only reason they had to try to "jump" the interview at the last-minute on the red carpet was no doubt through a lack of planning and organisation in the first place. If they had asked for an interview the day before, I am sure they would have been granted one, just like the others.

The lessons that can be gleaned from this example? Don't think you're bigger than your boots... or smaller. It doesn't matter who you are working for. Play by the rules, be polite, be organised, be professional, and be humble.

A good example of the other side of the coin was also at the World Music Awards. This time in Las Vegas in 2004. Being in Vegas, the show was huge. At the Thomas and Mack Center, where the awards took place, we had to cater for colossal media egos, with all the world's top TV channels vying for "the best" place on the red carpet, and a star list that was ridiculous it was so long... including Pamela Anderson, Marc Anthony, Kobe Bryant, Kelly Clarkson, David Copperfield, Clive Davis, Céline Dion, Michael Douglas, Hilary Duff, Josh Groban, Hoobastank, Whitney Houston, La Toya Jackson, Alicia Keys, Heidi Klum, Patti LaBelle, Avril Lavigne, Courtney Love, Maroon 5, Usher Raymond, Seal, Anna Nicole Smith, Kanye West... the list went on. As for the other editions, as the stars arrived, all the media were placed on the red carpet, depending, to some extent, on their global importance. During the show itself, they set-up in the media room next to the main hall, where the stars came to give "press calls" throughout the event. That means they posed for photos with their award, and briefly answered journalists' questions about how they felt winning their prize and so on.

There was one exception. A very quietly spoken, pleasant young woman – Kwala Mandel – representing People Magazine, took some time to explain to me – in the run up to the event – that she really would like to, or indeed NEEDED to get some "special" one-on-one interviews. She was not pushy. She just made me understand how important it was for her to have some very exclusive stuff. If it was the same content as everyone else, it wouldn't cut it. Not for People magazine.

I introduced her to the organisers, and together it was agreed that she would be the only journalist backstage during the entire show. Of course, the idea of getting great coverage in People was advantageous for everyone. But Kwala's attitude was what took her the extra mile. We also couldn't allow a pushy, aggressive journalist to hassle artists backstage just before they performed. As it turned out, Kwala was as polite, charming and amiable with the artists backstage as she was with everyone else. By being friendly, respectful, professional, but persuasive, she left the show with a truckload of stories that no one else could have had.

People ran a huge spread on the show. Everyone won: the artists, the organisers and the magazine. Needless to say, at the following year's show in Hollywood, Kwala was "VIP media" yet again, and has remained a good friend and confidante to this day.

Preparing for the interview

In an ideal world, all interviews should be thoroughly researched in order that you know WHY you're asking each question. Someone once said that you should know what the answers will be before you ask the questions. In some cases, that's true. At least you should know what kind of answer you might get, but it would be a boring world if we knew all the answers to all the questions beforehand. It's vital to understand the background of the person you are interviewing, the current news about them, and of course, above all, the reason or reasons you are doing the interview.

The way you conduct the interview will also depend largely on the media for which you are doing it. Plan beforehand what length the interview should be.

There is nothing more frustrating and time consuming than cutting down a 45-minute interview to five minutes or 650 words. If you are doing the interview with the aim of having one or two short grabs (say, 30 seconds or a minute each) for a video, let the person know that this is how you will be using the answers. If they are experienced, they will adapt accordingly and will make your job a lot easier in the end. They will also not be surprised that if they have rambled for 20 minutes, you have only used a very small part of what they said.

I witnessed the best case of this in 1984, when Peter Garrett, the singer of the famed rock band Midnight Oil, was campaigning to enter parliament. He came to Lismore where I was working at the time for 2LM, and I had the chance to interview him for our news. He knew the interview was for news, so for each question I asked, he gave me perfectly, beautifully structured answers of almost exactly 30 seconds. No umms or ahhhs, no hesitation. After each question, he thought for a second or two – time to structure his thoughts – and delivered an impeccably structured answer. He was (and still is) indeed an absolutely brilliant man in many ways, and I was thrilled and honoured to have met him.

At 2UE, we also had a cricket commentator who had the same gift. "How many seconds do you want?", he would ask. Depending on our needs, whether it was 30 or 40 seconds, he would ad-lib his report exactly to time. Very few people can do that. I know I can't.

Ask open questions

Take care to generally ask open questions; that is to say ones that can't be answered with a "yes" or a "no". I have occasionally heard interviewers ask questions which were so long that they answered themselves. Questions need to be short and to the point, and not multifaceted. Clarity in a question will help obtain a clear answer – although not always.

For example, rather than asking someone if they are angry or sad (closed), ask them how they feel. Rather than ask whether they want to increase their profits, ask them what outcome they are looking for from their current activities.

Look your interviewee in the eye

Be GENUINELY interested in what they have to say. Even though you may be looking at your notes to remember what the next question will be, listen attentively to what they are saying. If there are points that don't seem clear, ask them to elaborate. If, in their answer, they have touched upon a point you were not aware of, and that may add interest to the story if expanded upon, go back to that and get them to talk more about it. Don't just go on to your next question because that's what's written in your notes.

Don't ask highly technical questions just to prove you are up on the subject. It may boost your ego, but the readers or listeners will not be impressed.

Just in case there is something you may have forgotten, but the interviewee is dying to talk about, it can be very useful at the end of an interview to wrap up by saying, *"Is there anything else you'd like to mention that we haven't covered?"* It might be they have something brand new to talk about that even by researching you may not have found, and now you have a scoop.

Don't jump in

Avoid the temptation to jump in at the end of your interviewee's sentence. It may not have been his or her last sentence. They may simply be collecting their thoughts. When possible, leave a pause after what seems like the end of your interviewee's answer, as occasionally they will add a "pearl", having had time to think. There is a secondary effect here. When there is a "pregnant pause", your interviewee will feel obliged to talk about… well… anything – in order to fill the void with what could well be some very nice material for your story!

Covering all bases

Unless for a short "grab", an interview can often best be done based on the five W's +H (Who, what, when, where, why… and how). An example, if talking about a project, would be as follows:

Who was behind the project?

What exactly is it?

When did you decide to launch it, and what is the timeline for its completion?

Please tell us about where it is taking place…

What were the reasons behind its creation?

How is it being implemented?

Get down to the basics

Sometimes, the most simple, basic question can be the best one. A very general question will enable the interviewee to have some scope with their answer and go where THEY want to go.

This is, of course, if that's what you want them to do. Remember, you are the one asking the questions. You are in control.

A question like, "How's business going?", or "What does the roadmap look like for the next year or so?" enable the interviewee to say what they want to say about the most important points in their strategy.

"How IMPORTANT is…"

When you ask someone how important what they are talking about is, of course they will explain to you why it is important.

This will generally give you some good, strong content. It helps people put things in perspective. It can also be used in general news. For example, *"How important was this tsunami compared to others in the region over the past decades or centuries?"*

By the same token, it is rare that they would say *"It's not very important"*. To the contrary, most will give you an *"It's very important"* answer, meaning you can use that as a hook in your story (*"so-and-so says such-and-such is very important"*). In virtually all cases, the *"How important is…"* question will be useful.

"How do you FEEL about…"

Asking a question about how someone feels about a certain situation stimulates a part of the brain that creates a more emotive or emotional response.

"So how did that make you feel at the time?" – or one that always made me smile for race-winners: *"So you won a very tough race. How do you feel?"*

The answer is going to be pretty obvious, isn't it? But nevertheless, reporters always ask the same question. Indeed, while it IS obvious, the answer to this question is, in fact, the one people want to hear. *"I am elated. I've finally made it. This is the pinnacle..."* ... the list goes on.

The interviewee digs down into his or her soul and gives you a very emotional answer. If you come back with another "feeling" question the response can be even greater. A follow on (or lead-in) question/suggestion may be something like, *"You must have been very proud of that..."*, or *"That must have given you a great sense of satisfaction..."*

While these are closed questions, they can be part of a broader overall interview process that obtains the kind of result you are seeking.

You will note that in many interviews by the top "one-on-one" interviewers on top TV shows, these kinds of questions are very commonplace. This is why the interview turns out sounding very candid, and the subjects open up sometimes more than ever before.

Making the person feel important

If a person IS important, there is no harm in making them feel even more that way with a question about something that enables them to tell you why they are.

Again, here, you could say, *"I saw that yet again you have been awarded the prize of GM of the year... How did that make you feel?"*

In this case, you have flattered them, showed you have done some research, and are now playing to their emotions. They will feel much more open to following questions once you have enabled them to wax lyrical about their own prowess or the great achievements of their organisation.

Asking them about themselves

By asking a person they best way they could describe what they do, and where they're coming from (assuming now we are not talking about someone who is already well known), you are giving yourself some nice ammunition for the lead part of your story – leading into the interview. Re-work what they've said into an intro. For example, if, in an interview with winemaker Bill Bloggs, he says, *"I am quite happy, because I've been able to build up a strong reputation in just three years, since I've been chief winemaker for one of the top brands in Champagne."*

The story intro could read: *In the space of just three years, Bill Bloggs has become renowned for his work as a winemaker for one of the top Champagne brands in France. We asked him to tell us a little more about his background and how he landed in this position.*

In the case you actually don't know about the organisation (you have been thrown into the interview and have not had time to check), rather than ask about the organisation in a simple way, showing your ignorance, you could ask a question like, *"For those who are less familiar with your organisation, how would you best describe it in your words?"*

Asking the same question different ways

When an interviewee doesn't actually answer the question, don't hesitate to come back with it again, asked perhaps a little differently, or bring it back a little later in the conversation in a different way.

The interviewee has different reasons for not answering. Either they have not really understood – or their minds where elsewhere as you were asking, or they find it difficult and prefer to avoid answering.

In the case of politicians of course this is often the case, and they become experts at giving you a complex answer that has nothing at all to do with what you asked. You may even like to say, *"That's not really what I was asking. Actually, I would like to know XXXXX… Can you explain?"*

Keeping your cool

There may be times when you are interviewing someone that the tone starts to mount. The interviewee may become aggressively evasive or simply rude. It is much more effective in a situation like this to "keep your cool", and avoid being swept into the maelstrom.

A calm, informed approach can in fact be very disarming to a person who is trying to side-step a question through bluff and bullying tactics.

What are the "key selling points" of X?

This is always a good question to throw-in if you're doing a "commercial" interview (see the dedicated section on this). It makes the interviewer think, and can be a great conclusion or break-out. See also the section on key selling points.

Sure-fire questions

It can be interesting to throw in a slightly "intriguing" but sure-fire question. One that makes the person stretch out and think. These are "the old ones but the good ones":

If you had a time machine, and you could go back 20 years in time, but you could only stay a minute, what would Bill Bloggs of today say to Bill Bloggs of 20 years ago?

(For big bosses) – How would you best describe your management style?

How do you think your personnel would describe you if they were to be interviewed today?

What's the most challenging part of what you did? What kept you up at night?

What gives you the greatest satisfaction in your work?

What would you say gives you "the edge"?

What is the key to your success (or the success of this enterprise /

event / etc.)?

Why?

This is a good one. I learned it in the early 1980's from the then boss of 2CC, Nick Erby. In a conversation on any topic, he would get to a point where he would just say, *"Why?"*

Just one word. It punctuates the conversation and is very clear in its purpose. That is to say, you are telling me all this, but why?

Used in another way, it can pre-empt a strategic positioning. In that case, it would be, *"Why? (pause)... Why are you telling me about X when I asked you about Y?"*

A single word, or very short question has an incredible amount of power if delivered in the right way. It should only be used as a weapon when you feel the interviewee is really turning the discussion to his or her advantage for simple gain, or that they are trying to "get the upper hand".

Either way, it's not going well, because the ideal interview is a veritable exchange of ideas, with the proviso that YOU are the one setting the rules... so you have to re-assert yourself and let the interviewee know that you are the one "managing" the interview.

Avoid the blindingly obvious

It goes without saying... perhaps. But nevertheless, I occasionally see examples of this – in questions thrown-in by well-meaning journalists – probably when they are ad-libbing questions "on the hop". An example was a US TV interviewer speaking to a nurse during the early part of the Covid-19 pandemic - in April 2020. The killer question was, *"Have you ever seen anything like this before?"*

Now, really. You are a journalist. You know there has never been anything like this before in the US since, perhaps, the Spanish flu epidemic exactly a hundred years before. The likelihood that your nurse was around then, working as a nurse, is rather slim. Why not ask more interesting, probing questions that put her work in perspective, or give some sense of scale?

You could say, *"How exactly does this compare to previous epidemics?"* – to which she can better measure her answer. Yes, we know it's worse than the previous ones she would have dealt with... but to what degree?

Elicitation

If you are interviewing someone who you know may be "holding their cards close to their chest" – and you want to get them to open up, without asking direct questions, try using a technique which has become renowned thanks to the FBI in America. The organisation has successfully used elicitation over the years to get people to give up secret information in a very surreptitious manner.

Elicitation is defined by the FBI as "the strategic use of conversation to extract information from people without giving them the feeling they are being interrogated."

Elicitation is broadly outlined, among other things, by former FBI agent, Dr Jack Shafer, in his book "The Like Switch".

One kind of elicitation is based on the fact that all people have an automatic psychological tendency to correct people when they say something they know to be wrong. Indeed, people like to think they are right, but the need to correct someone else when they make a false statement is even greater. With elicitation, the idea is for the interviewer to make presumptive statements, thus prompting the interviewee to correct the statement.

Your presumptive statement (an educated guess), whether right or wrong, will generally prompt your interviewee to either confirm your presumption, or correct it, thus giving away their information.

If the statement is correct, the other person will assume you have in-depth knowledge and are an insider, will affirm the fact and often even give additional details. If, on the other hand, the presumptive statement is wrong, a person's need to correct kicks-in and they will often provide the correct answer accompanied by additional details.

In broader terms, elicitation is a conversation with a specific purpose: to collect information that is not readily available and do so without raising suspicion that specific facts are being sought. It is usually non-threatening, easy to disguise, deniable, and effective. This is why a large number of competitive business intelligence collectors and foreign intelligence officers are trained in elicitation tactics.

Following is a list of other common elicitation tactics, as outlined by, yes, the FBI, in a brochure which has been placed in the public domain (see reference in bibliography). Useful stuff, indeed...

Opposition / Feigned Incredulity: Indicate disbelief or opposition in order to prompt a person to offer information in defence of their position. *"There's no way you could design and produce this that fast!"* or *"That's good in theory, but..."*

Provocative Statement: Entice the person to direct a question toward you, in order to set up the rest of the conversation. *"I could kick myself for not taking that job offer."* Response: *"Why didn't you?"* Since the other person is asking the question, it makes your part in the subsequent conversation more innocuous.

Quote Reported Facts: Reference real or false information so the person believes that bit of information is in the public domain. *"Will you comment on reports that your company is laying off employees?"* *"Did you read how analysts predict..."*

Word Repetition: Repeat core words or concepts to encourage a person to expand on what he/she already said. *"3,000 metre range, huh? Interesting."*

Assumed Knowledge: Pretend to have knowledge or associations in common with a person. *"According to the computer network guys I used to work with…"*

Bracketing: Provide a high and low estimate in order to entice a more specific number. *"I assume rates will have to go up soon. I'd guess between five and 15 dollars."* Response: *"Probably around seven dollars."*

Can you top this? Tell an extreme story in hopes the person will want to top it. *"I heard Company M is developing an amazing new product that is capable of …"*

Confidential Bait: Pretend to divulge confidential information in hopes of receiving confidential information in return. *"Just between you and me…"* *"Off the record…"*

Criticism: Criticise an individual or organisation in which the person has an interest in hopes the person will disclose information during a defence. *"How did your company get that contract? Everybody knows Company B has better engineers for that type of work."*

Deliberate False Statements / Denial of the Obvious: Say something wrong in the hopes that the person will correct your statement with true information. *"Everybody knows that process won't work—it's just a DARPA dream project that will never get off the ground."*

Feigned Ignorance: Pretend to be ignorant of a topic in order to exploit the person's tendency to educate. *"I'm new to this field and could use all the help I can get."* *"How does this thing work?"*

Flattery: Use praise to coax a person into providing information. *"I bet you were the key person in designing this new product."*

Good Listener: Exploit the instinct to complain or brag, by listening patiently and validating the person's feelings (whether positive or negative). If a person feels they have someone to confide in, he/she may share more information.

The Leading Question: Ask a question to which the answer is "yes" or "no," but which contains at least one presumption. *"Did you work with integrated systems testing before you left that company?" (As opposed to: "What were your responsibilities at your prior job?")*

Macro to Micro: Start a conversation on the macro level, and then gradually guide the person toward the topic of actual interest. Start talking about the economy, then government spending, then potential defence budget cuts, then *"what will happen to your X programme if there are budget cuts?"* A good elicitor will then reverse the process taking the conversation back to macro topics.

Mutual Interest: Suggest you are similar to a person based on shared interests, hobbies, or experiences, as a way to obtain information or build a rapport before soliciting information. *"Your brother served in the Iraq war? So did mine. Which unit was your brother with?"*

Oblique Reference: Discuss one topic that may provide insight into a different topic. A question about the catering of a work party may actually be an attempt to understand the type of access outside vendors have to the facility.

Quid Pro Quo

In some interviews, you might be able to use quid pro quo. In other words, if you have some information that might be valuable for the interviewee... anything at all... then this could win you brownie points and earn you better quality responses.

An example of this came when I was touring Asia

around 2010 doing some face-to-face interviews and gathering information for IFA International - the official show daily of Europe's biggest consumer electronics trade event. My assistant had requested a meeting and interview with the President of a huge Korean electronics company (not naming names). The reply came back that we could have an interview with the Vice President, as the President didn't have time for an interview, but that on the other hand, the President would like to have tea with me in his board room before the interview with his VP. Arriving at their offices, we were ushered, along with the VP I was to interview, another VP, and various other senior staff, into the board room for tea with the President. As I sat facing him, he said he was very happy that I had come to visit his company HQ, and asked how many other HQs I had been visiting in Korea, Japan and China.

"Quite a few, as you can imagine," I answered, sipping at my green tea.

"What have you seen that was interesting?" he asked.

It instantly dawned on me. Here was me, an international journalist, touring his competitors.

Who better to ask what was going on? His staff certainly couldn't get the same visibility I had.

HE was interviewing ME.

I knew I had to be guarded with my answers, and keep them wholly within the realms of what I would be presenting in my articles – even if I HAD seen and heard things he would have liked to have known.

Nevertheless, I knew that the information I was giving him was still very valuable. And in return, he did give over some important snippets of information about changes to his strategy and overall company structure. Needless to say, the interview with his VP following this went very well.

In a situation like this, it is essential not to give away too much – for several reasons – not the least of which is the fact that if you blurt out secret information about a competitor, the person in front of you will NEVER give you any valuable information, in the knowledge that you may well do the same thing with HIS information.

If and when it is time to publish sensitive information, if it may be damaging for a company, you had better be sure your legal advisor has checked on the validity of the news in terms of public interest in order to avoid any legal hassles.

Over time, you will often be given information which is best kept unpublished and unsaid if you want to keep your contacts and your friends.

Lifestyle questions

In "lifestyle" interviews, you are not aiming to probe people in the same way as you might in a political, or "hard hitting" interview. In this kind of interview, your scope is broadened, and creativity steps in. Pretty much anything goes, within a framework of good taste and... fun. Lifestyle interviews aim to make people talk about themselves.

Asking about what they see as their greatest strengths and weaknesses, what keeps them up at night, what they wanted to be when they were little, what sports they practice, their hobbies, etc., are all part of the typical panoply of questions.

Try to step outside the box and find some different, amusing questions, or some that really make the person delve into their persona and reveal him or herself in a way that hasn't been done before. Again, here, a very personable, fun, friendly interview style is needed to get the best from people.

Be confident in your own questions

If you have thought through your questions, and you have

good reason for asking them, stand by your guns and don't be intimidated in the rare case that someone knocks one back at you. That is of course unless you didn't do your homework correctly and they're picking you up on something. THAT's embarrassing. But even then, remain steadfast and confident.

You are in charge of the interview. A good example of what I'm talking about happened the year Michael Schumacher had been crowned Formula One World Champion for the seventh time. At the end of the season, the annual FIA gala was set to take place in Monaco at the Summer Sporting Club; an event attended by all the teams and drivers. I received a call from a TV production company for whom I worked regularly, who were commissioned by Eurosport to cover the event.

"They need someone to interview Schumie on the red carpet when he arrives. We thought of you. They already have one key question they want to ask."

So, there I was on the red carpet, with Eurosport's hot little question in my hand. It was *"How, after winning more championships and races than anyone else, are you motivated to carry on?"*

I thought the question was pretty pertinent. On the red carpet, as people bowl by, you only get one hit. Just one question. This was it.

When Schumacher arrived, he was directed to talk to me; the camera was rolling, and I let fly with "the" question. He looked at me for what seemed like several minutes... but was probably several seconds, and said *"Everyone is asking me the same question. Don't you have another one?"*

"If everyone is asking you the same question, it's because that's what people want to know," I parried. *"It's the one we need the answer to."*

He gave me a wry smile. I'd got him. *"I love winning. I just want to keep winning. That's all..."* he admitted. He didn't need more motivation than that. When you're at the pinnacle, where do you go? In his case, you keep going as far as you can, creating a new pinnacle. That was the answer we wanted.

Schumie wasn't a hard man to interview. But he, like many others at a very high level in their field, knew "where he was at", and was clear with his thoughts at all times. I did in fact interview him at other times when I did some TV work for Ferrari (also via the production company in Monaco), and while he was perhaps a little timid or introverted at times, I found him to be very personable and pleasant.

What can seem like abrupt manner needs occasionally to be analysed, with each situation put into perspective. Working also on TV production for the World Endurance Championship (the championship surrounding the 24 Hours of Le Mans), I noted this in particular with Mark Webber, the former Formula One driver who was then driving quite successfully for Porsche. While never impolite, he always seemed to be a bit "rushed".

One of the things we would do at each race would be to get a top-line driver to comment a lap of the circuit, as seen from the driver's seat. Rather than rig up a microphone while the driver was doing a lap, we would take the on-board images from his car, playing them back on a PC later in the day in the driver's motorhome or catering area, while he commented each gear change, braking zone, corner and acceleration as they happened. We would then sync the audio with the images, and it sounded to all intents and purposes like the driver was commenting from behind the wheel. The first time I went to record the audio with Mark Webber, I said, *"Do you want to quickly run through the video first?"*

"Nope. Just run it. She'll be right!", he said.

I did, he commented the lap word perfect, then stood up and said, *"There you go. See ya."*

Hmmm. It was faultless. It dawned on me that this was one of the reasons someone like Mark was such an amazingly good driver. His concentration on any single task was instant, perfectly dosed, well-organised, and thus brief. This was part of the job, which had to be totally efficient, in every way. The year Mark retired, just after the last race, we met in the lobby of the Bahrain Sofitel as the teams were arriving for the end of season bash. It was a very different Mark this time. Relaxed and chatty. Work was over. Yes indeed, at the track, work had been work. Serious work.

An interview for a monologue

Sometimes, quotable quotes can be presented as monologues, rather than in interview format. In this case, your task will be to broadly brief the person you are interviewing as to the aim of your piece, and then just get them to talk. You should have in mind how long the piece will be before getting the person to expand eternally on a point, to avoid unnecessary editing afterwards. Some interviews will be very easy to edit, and some will be hellish.

A good example was in 1999, when I worked with the star German photographer Vanessa Von Zitzewitz on a 256-page book called Monachrome, published by Giorgio Mondadori. The book was a coffee-table collection of dozens upon dozens of famous people – from all walks of life – living in Monaco, with breath-taking black-and-white photos by Vanessa accompanied by a monologue from each of the subjects, outlining their hopes and dreams for the new millennium. Interviewees included Claudia Schiffer, Fernando Botero, Ringo Starr, Monica Bellucci, Fabien Barthez, Shirley Bassey, Andrei Medvedev, Jacques Villeneuve, Alberto Tomba, Karen Mulder, Roger Moore, Helmut Newton, Luciano Pavarotti, Mick Doohan, Gerhard Berger, Jean-Michel Folon, Guido Cappellini, Ari Vatanen, Sacha Sosno, Ursula Andress, Alain Ducasse, and Adami. 100% of sales of the book were donated to the Monegasque Red Cross, who, by the way, do an incredible job, and largely deserved the rather large cheque Vanessa and I presented to Prince Albert II of Monaco – the official head of the association.

My job was to interview the subjects and turn the resulting answers into the desired monologues for the book. Some were easy. A few – those who felt comfortable doing so – wrote their own monologues. But most of the monologues came from interviews. I think the longest was with French footballer Fabien Barthez – maybe half an hour. Getting that down to a couple of sentences took me ages. But that said, the condensation of what he said into a single statement turned out to be very strong, whereas a single, short, ill-thought-out statement from him would not have transmitted the true depth of what he was trying to say. In the case, like this, of a footballer, we should not forget that the person never trained to be an orator, but may well have thoughts and ideas that are deep and interesting.

Editing

Editing down a really great interview is very frustrating. Space is generally limited, unless you're running a long online version of the interview. You will generally find yourself confronted with the dilemma of which great quotes you are going to have to cut out in order to get the interview down to size. In all cases, remember that the reader or listener has no knowledge of these bits, and will find it interesting in any case. If you have some flexibility in a publication, you may be able to expand the space if your interview is really dynamite.

For print, it can be necessary to rework the structure and language of an interview in order for it to make sense. Some of the most brilliant people I interview go off on tangents or ramble. Paraphrasing this back into something that is well structured is part of our job. It often happens as well that an interviewee will come back to a subject he or she spoke about five minutes before – expanding on the previous details. In that case, take the two parts and put them together in the written text – making the interview much more coherent.

In some cases where I may totally transform what was said (while attempting to retain a certain amount of the "style" of the interviewee), I will generally check it back with them to see if he or she is in agreement with what I have done, as their name and reputation are at stake.

When properly reworking an interview, you are generally doing the interviewee a big favour, making them sound a lot better than in real life, and going straight to the heart of what they were trying to convey all along. Perhaps the most flattering feedback I had on something like this was from Matthew Upchurch, CEO and Chairman of the ultra-luxury Virtuoso travel advisors' network a few of years ago. I interviewed Matthew, an eloquent, highly intelligent and forthright man, for the quarterly Hotel and Tourism SMARTreport. The interview was "on the spot" at the International Luxury Travel Market (ILTM) in Cannes, where I asked him if he had a few minutes for a chat. He said, *"Yes, but I don't have much time, as I have an appointment coming up."*

I told him that was fine, and we proceeded to begin discussing his philosophy and how this made Virtuoso different. He was totally impassioned by this; it was obvious. What he was saying made a lot of sense, and was truly an eye-opener for me. I could sense that he knew I was totally on his wavelength. There were no set questions; it was a discussion.

Almost an hour later, with Matthew pushing back his standing appointments, I left with a remarkable, but amazingly complex interview. In this particular case, my theory of keeping an interview roughly to the length of what it will be used for was not going to work. In the end, we ran two pages (around 900 words) in the next edition, and another two pages in the following one, as a "part two", because there was so much to tell. Even so, editing this was a huge job. I needed to write what Matthew was trying to say without losing the passion, the energy, and some of the most important anecdotes. The following year, I was invited to Virtuoso Travel Week in Las Vegas, where Matthew presented me to his members as *"the one who had found his voice".*

A greater complement would be very hard to find. In cases like this, it's win-win, as the interviewee's views are presented in a way that he or she greatly appreciates, and for us, we have content that is truly exceptional for our readers.

Intro structure

The intro to an interview can be done in several ways. It is, in all cases, important to "paint the picture" of what you will be talking about in the space of a sentence or two. If you are doing an intro for a video or audio interview, there are two main ways to throw to the interview. In the first, after a brief one- or two-paragraph introduction, the text may read: *"We asked Company X CEO Bill Bloggs what he thought of the situation,"* followed by Bill Bloggs explaining that the situation is untenable.

Using a more modern style, the text would read: *"Company X CEO Bill Bloggs says he feels the situation is untenable."* – followed by the rest of the interview.

In the first case, we have the punchy sentence of Bill Bloggs saying the situation is untenable. The second, however, flows and reads more easily. I also tend to use this style in written form, as I also think it reads better.

Rather than putting the person's name or initials at the start of each answer, it is rote that the answers are always from the same person, so we put the questions in bold italics, and the answers in normal type.

On the other hand, when two people are interviewed side by

side, we do put the initials of each one next to their answers. Be careful not to run a "dual" interview where it is not clear who is answering what question. More than once, we have received press releases quoting two people for an entire interview. Unless they had rehearsed and sung or chanted it together, it just wouldn't happen.

Interviews by email

More and more people like to do press interviews by email. It enables them to have time to weigh-up and consider each question. It also avoids you having to tediously type-up the answers. On the other hand, however, as your interviewee rarely will be someone accustomed to writing in this way, the interview can well turn out to be sterile, staged and even boring.

Worse, if a PR company becomes involved, they may attempt to turn the interview into a veiled advertisement, with sentences cut and pasted from promotional brochures. For this reason, when possible, always try to do the interview in person – either face to face, or in a worst-case scenario, by phone. When an interview is done by email, you will generally have a major editing job to do to turn it into something that actually looks like an interview. In other words, as you are reading it, you should be able to imagine that person saying the words... not writing them. While avoiding poor English, this is nevertheless an important factor in turning an interview like this around.

One such interview I received a couple of years ago came from the president of a very major US corportation. We'd gone through their PR firm in New York for the interview, and they acted entirely as the intermediary. I generally don't like this, but in this case, there was no choice. We sent our questions, and explained we were looking for around 1200 words, which equated to three pages in the publication. We indeed received around 1200 words, but the interview ended up taking only two pages by the time I'd cut out all the publicity blah-blah that someone at the agency had copied from the website. If at all possible, avoid going through PR people for these kinds of interviews.

Another death knell of an interview sent back in a word file is that of bullet points or numbered points in an answer. The written interview, despite being written, needs to at least give the IMPRESSION of being a real conversation with someone. Yes, we correct the grammar and often the language and structure as well, to make the interviewee "sound" better, but in a real conversation, no one actually talks with bullet points. When someone sends you a bullet point answer, paraphrase the answer into a series of points separated by semi-colons or commas (depending what is said and how it is said). The same goes for brackets. People don't talk with brackets, so they shouldn't be included in interview text.

Timing

As previously mentioned, when doing a written interview based on recorded answers, it is very important, especially when working to deadline or with other time constraints, to time your interview in such a way that it is just a tiny bit longer than the desired length of your text. The average person utters around 120 words a minute, so if your text is set to 1,000 words, anything longer than ten or twelve minutes is going to cause you to spend more time on cutting and editing than on writing. The exception to this rule is if you really feel you haven't gleaned what you want from your subject, and you need to dig a little deeper. Otherwise, before doing the interview, be aware of how long you will want the text to be, and try to time your interview to fit.

Recorded or shorthand?

If you are lucky enough to have shorthand, that's great – especially for taking notes in a press conference, in court, in a council meeting, a political debate … the list goes on. When I do not believe it is useful is in the case of an interview for print media. Even if you are going to have to edit your interview, it is extremely important to make an audio recording, which, in case of doubt over the sense of an answer, will be your best defence. It is also important, even if the interview is edited, to keep the spirit and style of the interviewee, which is often very individual. Some people have specific phrases or sayings that are their trademarks. It is best that these be reproduced as they are said. It's more difficult if the interview is based on scribbled notes. Furthermore, the fact of having to concentrate on writing as the interviewee is speaking takes away from your capacity to be thinking about your next question or questions. Indeed, even though you may have begun with a set series of questions, a surprising answer SHOULD lead you to ask a different question to the one that was originally planned, or at least to alter what you had planned. By recording, your mind is free – not only to listen intently to the answers – but also to consider changes or additions to your line of questioning.

You are not the star

It's not about you. It's about your interviewee. On TV, or in video blogs, often the interviewer insists on being in the image all the time in a "two-shot". Just get over yourself and realise it's not like this that you are going to become a star. The people you are talking to are the ones the people watching the screen want to see. If you are on screen for a stand-up or to explain things, that's different. But in an interview, your subject is the one that should be on the screen most of the time.

Find a cool, interesting setting for your interview... or at least a quiet one

What about side-by-side on a pair of chaises longues on the pier of the Carlton Hotel in Cannes – for an interview with a famous Australian film producer (my old, late, friend David Hannay)?

Or a radio interview with racing ace Stirling Moss, driving around Lakeside Raceway in Brisbane at very high speed, with me in the passenger's seat?

If you're not looking for effect, try to make sure the place is pleasant, and quiet, and that there are as few distractions as possible.

Dress for the part

How many times have I seen a poorly dressed, dishevelled reporter interviewing a company president, politician or other "leader", who is dressed to the nines? Reporters often tell me that AS they are journalists, everyone knows they dress that way, and so it's okay. It's not.

If you dress like a tramp, the person being interviewed, while not commenting on your look, will subliminally feel you are inferior in some way; not because you dress in a casual way, but because the fact you are dressed in a casual way in a formal environment indicates a kind of contempt or disrespect.

While you don't have to dress exactly the same way as your interviewee, do make an effort to dress similarly. If you know they will be wearing a suit, do wear at least a smart jacket (if you are a guy), or a business-like outfit of some kind if you are woman. If you are attending an event where everyone wears ties, wear a tie (guys). If it's black tie, wear a black tie.

By the same token, if you turn up for an interview "dressed up", and the interviewee is dressed casually, try to adapt if you can.

NEWS AND
ADVERTISING

In any media organisation, there tends to be a kind of love-hate relationship between people working in the advertising department and those working in news. The ad people know that what they sell depends on the quality of the news, and the news people know that without the ads, they wouldn't have a job. The appreciation often stops there, with snide jokes often made across a kind of battle-line, one making fun of the other, whenever possible.

When first working on air in commercial radio – at 2BS Bathurst, the owner, Ron Camplin explained to me why, to his mind, ads were good, and why he loved having LOTS of ads on air: *"A radio ad is good when it gives someone useful information about something that is close to their heart. For example, learning that a sale is on at a certain store, with jeans at half price, is useful information for someone in the market for jeans. People are actually very interested in getting information about what's going on around them in this way."*

This explains why most of the ads on his station at that time were in fact very "informational", rather than being just brand marketing. Indeed, local media still play an important role in this way.

Yes, both news and advertising convey information that is

useful – in different ways – to the reader, listener or viewer. They are also often structured in a similar way, as the catch phrase or slogan in an ad is in fact its headline. Seen the other way around, a headline and first paragraph of a news story should be as punchy, catchy and informative as in an ad.

Having worked in radio news for around six years in Australia, when I travelled to Europe, I ended up working in radio (and occasionally TV) advertising sales, copywriting and production in Monaco for around seven years, before working in print advertising, then moving back across the battle-line into print and TV journalism. I was thus able to experience, first hand, the similarities and synergies between these two worlds. Here are just a few:

Human contact: A good journalist must have an exceptional ease of contact with people, and must also be an ace at networking. People need to trust you totally with their information. They need to be friends… real friends. This is not a fake "How ARE you?", but a circle of people who start as contacts and become more than that. In advertising, the concept is very similar. Someone who knows and trusts you will be much more likely to invest part of their budget thanks to your advice. They will also be likely to take your advice about how they should present their message, if they have not already thought that one through (as often they haven't).

Information gathering: For both advertising and news, all information needs to be gathered in a logical and methodical way. Facts need to be checked and details should not be overlooked. Quite often, the most pertinent, pithy fact, that will make the difference in a news story or an ad, are dredged-up after a long conversation with the client or the news contact. It's that "ahhh" moment: "Ahhh, that's the story. That's the news." All the rest is support material, but the lead was buried down in the guff. In advertising, a good copywriter has exactly the same task - find "the lead".

Information structure: Headline or catch-phrase, both need to grab the attention of the reader, listener or viewer in the space of two or three seconds. This can either be done through a very basic, unambiguous statement that explains what this is all about, or, to the contrary can be enigmatic, again spawning interest, and generally – in print - leading the reader's eye to the sub-heading which is less ambiguous. The overall structure of a news story or ad are basically the same, albeit that an ad generally tends to be much shorter. That said, this doesn't have to be the case – particularly when it comes to advertorial, which is basically paid editorial content, with an evident slant towards the advertiser. In an ad, the first thing to hit the audience can either be a call to action based upon the potential buyer's needs, or simply what the company is selling or doing – <u>not</u> the name of the company. Print advertorial should always be clearly marked as such, but should also fit in with the style – both editorial and artistic – of the publication.

Visuals: The visual material in either an ad or a news story need to be totally pertinent and of excellent quality. That's where the similarity generally stops. Advertisements will tend to have visuals that exaggerate the quality and design aspect of the product, while in news – especially in commercial (B2B) news, photos or charts will be visual support for the article or interview – and much more "matter of fact". While they need to be attractive and professional in nature, they aim to be instructive rather than just "sell" a product.

3 key selling points: a lesson from another past

At the age of 19, having dropped out of a science degree course at Newcastle University in Australia, I found work in the menswear department of Myer Bathurst – the closest town to our then home in New South Wales. The store manager was Nevil Barlow, also Mayor of Bathurst; a very sharp and wise man who also made his presence felt in the store. He insisted on staff training as one of the ways to give us "the edge". One of the key lessons was that of the "three key selling points". I prefer "key" selling point to "unique" selling point, which means it's the only one of its kind: generally, that's not the case. Unique tends to be a word that is grossly overused – as outlined the style section. For example, having exceptional quality of production could be said to be a key selling point, but it is not unique in itself.

We were instructed that we should learn the three main points or differentiation points of every single item we were selling, whether it be a pair of socks, a tie-pin, a shirt, a three-piece suit, or a pair of underpants. *"If you can't give me three reasons that help me understand why this pair of socks, at five dollars, is better for me than the ones next to them – that look similar – at two dollars – then I will buy the ones for two dollars. But if you explain to me that thanks to their stretch design, they are much more comfortable; thanks to the fine cotton from India, they breathe better; and thanks to the quality of manufacturing, they will last at least twice as long as the others, of course I will buy the more expensive ones, and be happier with them."*

The concept just made sense, and it worked.

Even today, many of the concepts and ideas that were imparted in those weekly coaching sessions in Bathurst – that were in fact part of the overall Myer store training state-wide, have stayed stuck, to the point that when I go into stores today, I wish the staff there had the same kind of training in order to give them the tools to communicate in the right way with me – now the customer. Yes, it was all about how to communicate the right way, in order to sell.

It wasn't until many years later, in fact, around 2010, that one of the key lessons from that time became a part of my new routine. As publishers of IFA International, the official show daily at IFA Berlin – arguably the world's most important consumer electronics and home appliance trade show, one of our key tasks was to present the plethora of new devices being released at the event and to help our readers put them, and the companies making them, into perspective. The magazine did not target members of the general public, but directly reached out to the over 100-thousand trade visitors at the show. These were often buyers operating for big retail chains, and who made decisions, based on what they saw at this show, as to how many tens of thousands of TVs they would buy from Samsung, LG, Panasonic, Sony, TCL, and so on, not to mention mobile devices, headphones, drones, fridges, washing machines, coffee makers, foot warmers… the list was almost endless. In the space of a few days, five or six billion euros worth of orders would be signed.

Choosing correctly means making the difference between your stores, that will have the right stock on the shelves in time for Christmas, as opposed to your competitors, who maybe didn't do their homework right, and will lose out in sales. An important part of this process is what we called "information intelligence". That is to say, getting the right information at the right rime in order to make the right decisions. Our magazine thus played a pivotal role in the decision-making process.

After producing the daily for a few years, we decided to add "buyers' guides" to our pages, helping these big retail buyers in their decision-making process thanks to concise, pertinent and sometimes visionary information from some of the top experts in the field – primarily from EISA – the European Image and Sound Association. So, what were we looking for? Memories of those days in the little training room at Myers came back to me. Of course – three key selling points. We needed to explain what the three most important selling points were to look for in a certain item – whether it be a fridge, TV, radio, wireless speaker… whatever. As these devices change quickly over time, what are the three main points to look for?

Why three? People may wonder why three is the "magic" number when it comes to key selling points. Often, companies will give a list of eight or ten selling points for a product. At a trade show, when people are bombarded with massive amounts of information, it is impossible to grasp and remember that number of reasons as the primary differentiators of a product (or even company). When we introduced "three key selling points" to help describe products, the feedback was terrific. Buyers liked it. It made it easy to see the difference between six or seven different products in a double-page spread, without having to read all the details. Afterwards, when the buyers had more time, they could get down to the nitty-gritty, but at a first glance, the key selling points stood out much like headlines, and were very easy to remember.

Thus, when interviewing product managers or marketing bosses, we asked, "What are the three key selling points of this item?". Many found it difficult to answer, and had to think for a long time before dredging out a few ideas. They just failed the Myer sales course.

In the years following the introduction of the "three key selling points" concept to a great number of our articles and interviews in IFA International, the idea dawned on us. As we were also publishing the official magazines of the world's biggest travel and tourism show – ITB Berlin, and the world's most important wine shows – Vinexpo Bordeaux and Hong Kong – could this concept be transferred to those fields as well? Well, yes it could. Every trade show is about selling products. In the case of a travel and tourism show, the product may be a destination, a new hotel or resort, an airline, or the services of a tour operator. At the wine shows, of course people are selling primarily one kind of product: wine. So how can a buyer understand why to buy one "product" rather than another? Why should a travel agent who is attending ITB Berlin sign one new resort in Bali onto his books rather than another that has a similar star-rating and looks alike?

Here again, when interviewing sales and marketing people,

one of the questions we would always ask is "What are your destination's (or hotel's, or airline's, etc.) three "key selling points"? What are the three elements or factors that set you apart? Once we had these from different players in the market, we could then present them on the page in a separate break-out box that helped the buyers (again, people who are often signing for many millions of Euros in orders) make the right decision. It was information intelligence. It made finding, understanding and remembering the information much easier, and made the information instantly useable, as THEY could then see how THEY could sell the products.

In the field of travel, it is quite hard to find people who are able to explain this, as in general they have not thought along these lines. Again, they tend to have long lists of what's nice, or tell you they have white sandy beaches, swaying palms and blue seas... Well duh, so do ten thousand other resorts. But what makes YOURS different? Often, we would do the job for them. This was a task of analysis, and thus somewhat different from the kind of journalism where you simply reproduce what you're told, but it was a valuable addition to the articles.

In the world of wines, finding three key differentiators was even more important, as there are so many winemakers and wines on the market. Yet again, when asked the question, the result was often a blank look for some seconds before answers were forthcoming. In this sense, our means of communication approaches advertising, but that is for a very good reason. Simple, clear messages that could move people to action were part of the way we were communicating. These were of course complemented with more detailed information, either in the form of an interview, or a report or feature article.

Commercial journalism: filling a need that wasn't there before

In the world of commercial journalism, one can live from

writing stories for established publications, or even new ones in well-established fields of interest. On the other hand, much like Apple with the iPhone, creating a product that filled a need that didn't exist before, this is also possible in the world of publishing; or in any case, filling needs that organisations or companies didn't know they had.

In our line of work, sometimes it is possible to create and fill a need that people didn't know existed in the first place.

Here is an example. In December 2014, I travelled to Brussels, where I met with the head of communication for the European Travel Commission (ETC) for a discussion about their content planning for the ITB Berlin show three months later. Our head of advertising asked me to ask him whether they had a budget for advertising, as they had the previous year. He told me there was no budget at all for advertising. For me, that was fine, and didn't change anything at all with regard to editorial content.

I asked him how they did allocate their budgets, to which he explained that his organisation had embarked on a whole series of presentations around the world – targeting travel agents and tour operators – outlining all the advantages of "Europe as a destination", as opposed to people visiting individual countries.

I asked what kind of collateral they gave these people after the presentations, and it turns out there was nothing specific made for this purpose.

"So, you do a whole presentation, but when the attendees go back to their offices and talk to their colleagues about what they saw, they have nothing specifically that reflects the presentation? What if we designed a kind of guide to do this, covering everything that's new… all you are talking about, so they have something solid to take with them?", I asked.

He agreed it was a good idea, and we designed a 32-page "SMARTguide" called "Travelling in Europe". The ETC was able to obtain funding for this from the European Commission as a marketing support. We produced the guide and it became an important part of the ETC's communication and marketing for some time.

Had I not asked the question about how they communicate, and suggested this solution, the guide would not have existed. We made something from nothing – where there was not even any demand. But once done, it was very useful for all concerned. Much like the iPhone, no one knew they needed one until it was invented.

This happens more regularly that one might think. And when it doesn't, it should. Most times, there are areas of mar-comm that are ignored or misunderstood and are just waiting for an original idea.

Crossing the boundary – custom publishing

Custom publishing blurs the lines between advertorial and editorial. Over the years, with the team at Cleverdis, we produced mini-publications that were entirely dedicated to one product, brand or manufacturer. By the same token, the editorial content was gathered in the same way as it was for any other publication. That's what gave it its value. If it were to appear as a 16- or 24-page advertorial, it would serve little purpose for the reader, who would not take it very seriously.

Are you a good sales-person?

If your answer is "no", you should think again. Working as a journalist means operating very much like a sales person. You have to sell yourself, your ideas, your magazine, newspaper, radio station or TV show... So being a good sales person is an essential element.

Much like a good sales person, you also need to build up your "source" contact list, talk to them on a regular basis or go out for drinks or meals with them in order to kindle the relationships.

On the other side, if you are freelancing, the "selling" also has to be done on the "buying" end. In that case, it really is selling.

Good journalists are always very gregarious, and many thus fall into the trap of alcoholism. It's important to keep control, but not always easy – especially when media "junkets" by big companies are made with the express idea of getting the media sloshed – and thus more apt to be on their good side.

Always remember you are representing a media organisation, and your reputation may be on the line if you take things too far. But organised and undertaken properly, socialising skills are essential in this business, just like they are in selling any other valuable product or service.

INFORMATION FLOW AND WORK PROCESSES

In different media, there are of course different kinds of information flow. While it's a bit of a dry topic, I think it will be useful for me to impart some ideas as to what has worked for me. I won't go into how it works with radio news, as it kind of goes without saying, and is relatively simple. For TV reporting, the job of the journalist is also relatively straightforward.

What has changed in the field of video over the past few years is that in many cases, the journalist is more "hands on" with the video material. Working on motorsport magazine programmes – such as the World Endurance Championship or the World Series by Renault, an interview done in the pit lane or the paddock would, a number of years ago, be brought back to the post production suite by the ENG cameraman where an editor would sit laboriously with the journalist and select the parts of the interview to be used for the final edit. Using analogue Beta tapes, the images would be transferred from one tape to another in a first edit, then again to another tape in the final edit. The journalist would never touch the controls. Which was a good thing for me, as I had no idea how they worked.

Today, using software such as Final Cut Pro, everything has

changed. This is how we worked at Le Mans, or for other World Endurance Series races:

The images are, as before, brought back to the post production suite by the cameraman – or, as the case may be, the cameraman may simply pass the SD card to the journalist and continue his work. The images are then "ingested" and placed in a hierarchical order on a (very big) central server. Once there, the journalist can simply open the program on his or her Mac (yes, always a Mac), access the images on the server, and very simply edit the interview.

This does not take away the job of the editor, who now is able to spend more time "dressing" the segment once the very basic edit is done by the journalist. Once all the clips, interviews, race segments and so on are finished, they all come together into a 26 or 52-minute programme ready to run – generally on the night after the actual race, meaning the concept of an eight-hour day is totally ridiculous for anyone working in this field. Many has been the time we have finished a programme, putting the voice-over on the different sections and doing the final audio mix as the sun is coming up... or later. Bullish tenacity, patience and copious quantities of energy drink and chocolate help one to get through in the end. A deadline is a deadline, and when a show has to go out to a network the day after the race (or other event), you have no choice but to deliver.

Working on trade show dailies is a lot more complex when it comes to work flow, where you have to produce hundreds of pages in a rather short space of time. Taking the example of IFA International – the official daily for one of the two biggest consumer electronics shows in the world, we produced a preview edition a week before the event, five live editions at the show and a review a week after the show. It has to be said that the first years of doing this were very much "seat of the pants", but the know-how we developed over the years, which came through necessity as the beast grew, enabled us to spread into numerous other fields, and to become specialists in this kind of publication.

Year by year, we developed systems that were increasingly efficient, albeit always perfectible.

As the system is constantly evolving, here I will cite an editorial information flow based on three main platforms: Trello.com, Flat-plan.com and Wordpress.

Trello is a *"Collaboration tool that organises your projects into boards. In one glance, Trello tells you what's being worked on, who's working on what, and where something is in a process. Imagine a white board, filled with lists of sticky notes, with each note as a task for you and your team. Now imagine that each of those sticky notes has photos, attachments from other data sources like BitBucket or Salesforce, documents, and a place to comment and collaborate with your teammates. Now imagine that you can take that whiteboard anywhere you go on your smartphone, and can access it from any computer through the web. That's Trello."*

That's in fact how Trello describes itself. And it's pretty accurate. When several people are contacting potential interviewees, clients, exhibitors and so on, requesting information, it is essential to have a tool like this so that different people can follow what's going on.

The flat plan is, for uninitiated, the overview of the page layout. Basically, what goes on what page. In the early days, we juggled between Excel files and Adobe InDesign, which was cumbersome, time consuming, and also meant that every time something was changed, a whole bunch of new flat plans would have to be printed. One associate editor we had, Bob Snyder, an American from the "old school" (the one I like), was known for crying out, *"Where is my chemin de furrrrr?"* The French call it a chemin de fer (like a railway) – no doubt something to do with keeping it all moving, I guess. It was always a stumbling point, and more we had pages, more it became tricky.

We finally came upon Flat-plan.com. It's an online interactive tool for making a chemin de furrrrr (the hangover name from Bob's days has stayed stuck). According to its makers, *"It is the most effective online flatplan tool available. It is designed for publications, especially magazines, but is also useful for smaller books and papers less than 1,000 pages. By using it, you can create a sheet which immediately displays your plan (articles, ads, titles, page numbers). If you want to instantly renumber pages or are fed up with clumsy file formats, forget about it! Flat-Plan will create your flatplan instead of you having to do all the work!"*

Information workflow

When handing a large amount of information in any publishing or broadcast organisation, work flow is an essential part of the process. It is absolutely vital for channelling the right information into the right place at the right time, and can be THE place where a media organisation fails – even though it has good journalistic staff. Here are a couple of examples of how we have handled work flow – in this case for commercial print media – but applicable for any other.

In the past, a cloud server such as Google Drive was used for creating a hierarchy for the actual movement of base material, texts, photos and so on from the start of the chain right up to being sent to the printers. It was also possible to do the same thing using a plug-in on WordPress called "Edit Flow" under the subheading "Custom Statuses".

Let's firstly look at how we moved information around using Google Drive. Each publication had its own folder on the drive; i.e. IFA International 2021. Within that folder we had database folders, one for ads, one for web-based material, and another "main" folder, covering everything from editing to printing. Within the main folder, we had separate folders for each day's edition. And for each day's edition, we had five folders:

"Work to journalists" – this is a folder into which the editorial coordinator placed work he or she had taken from the database – or otherwise may have just received – in sub-folders for the various journalists. The work folder would be named with the edition, the page number, the name of the article, and requested word count. These were verified on the flat plan. Once the journalist had written up the story, he or she placed it in...

"To Sub" – where a sub-editor picked it up, subbed it, and placed it in...

"Pre-Page Setting" – where the head of production checked all the elements were there, that they were all properly named, that the photo was of the right resolution and quality, and that the word count was right... and then it was passed on...

"To Page Setting" – where it was picked up by the page setting crew. They consulted the flat plan and went to work on setting the page, putting the base files in a "taken" folder, before sending the page-set single page high resolution PDF to...

"Page Setting Complete" – the final pages. From this folder, each file was printed, and placed into a hard copy "verification book", where a number of people would re-proof read the copy. Errors were corrected and a virtually complete version was printed ready for final checking by yours truly as editor in chief. Some pages went back for final, final touches before they were all signed off ready to print.

And then the process repeated itself the next day... and so on.

Similarly, in WordPress, using the "Custom Statuses" section of the Edit Flow plugin, we created different folders, such as "Pitch" (when a journalist pitches an article), "Assigned" (when an article is assigned to a specific journalist), "Draft" (waiting to be assigned), "To Sub" (speaks for itself), "Editorial Check" (if in need of a second check), "Pre-page-setting" (where head of production checks all elements are OK to send to page-setting),

"Pre-publish" (if waiting for an "OK to print" in the case of advertorial), "To publish" (ready to publish), and "Published".

What's important to retain in this is that interactive processes of these kinds are increasingly vital the bigger a publication becomes. Different organisations customise and adapt them to their own situations.

Naming files

It's a pet bugbear. Whatever the purpose of your file, whether it be a news text, a press release, a photo, or a written interview, put some thought into how you name it.

As editor-in-chief, people would often send me files labelled, "Interview", or "IFA text", or something of the like. Imagine, if you might, when we have hundreds of pages to produce in a short space of time, how useful that is for me if the file finds itself on my desktop. The first thing we generally have to do is rename files into something that actually says what they are. For photos, the lack of names is even more of a problem.

When you have numerous journalists and sub-editors accessing folders on a server to work on stories, if the accompanying portrait photo comes named with a nonsensical combination of letters and numbers, such as DSCF8157, there is a very good chance that a mistake will be made somewhere along the line. One of the first things to be done when receiving photos is thus generally to rename them before they can be pushed and pulled along the work chain. This is also the case for landscape photos. A photo of an elephant on a lake shore in Zimbabwe may arrive named "Elephant 1". But if, at a later date, we are working on a story about Zimbabwe, including "Zimbabwe" in the file name will be important. Where it is stored, how that folder is named, and its logical hierarchy within other folders, will be as well.

PRESS RELEASES

Press releases are often a source of news, and are often at the heart of our work. As a journalist, you may also go on to work in a PR company or big corporation one day, writing them, or perhaps you may become a parliamentary press secretary, writing material for a politician or a party, or work in the press department of a Ministry or state marketing organisation. In all cases, writing effective press releases will be essential.

While being editor-in-chief for a number of publications, as I was freelance, I would also occasionally work on press releases for major organisations.

In its basic form, a press release should be able to be taken simply by a (lazy) journalist and run as is, without rewriting or interpreting. On the media side, however, we quite often find press releases that leave us scratching our heads.

For a few years in the late 90s, I worked externally (part time) as a professor at IUT Sophia Antipolis (Nice University) working with third year students on creative writing and press releases. Much of this chapter is a recap of the kind of observations we made then and that continue to be true today.

Some of my most vivid memories of how important press releases can be came from the mid 1980s. An example was in early 1986, when I was working as breakfast desk editor at 4BC United Network News in Brisbane. The politician Charles

Blunt, whom I had come to know from my previous job at 2LM in Lismore, had moved up in the political world. Having only entered into politics in 1984 as the National Party Federal Member for Richmond in north-eastern New South Wales, he had just been named as the Shadow Minister for Social Security.

While, to be frank, our political views were totally opposed, I used to get on very well with Charles (as I did also with the then dictatorial ultra-right-wing Premier of Queensland, Joh Bjelke-Petersen). So, when a very long press release from Charles came across my desk in Brisbane, the first paragraph of which was so boring it would normally have condemned it to the "round file" (i.e. the garbage bin), I took the time to look all the way through it. Somewhere near the end, I discovered the actual key to the story he was trying to tell. I called him and told him the release was crap, and explained why.

The very next day, he called me. *"I've fired my press secretary. The job's yours if you want it,"* he said. He went through the lurks and perks that come with such a position, and I politely said no. While I could point out to him where his press person had messed up, I couldn't in all conscience sit down and write propaganda for the National party.

A couple of years prior to this, in 1984 (not too long after Charles's wonderful quadruple tautology in his maiden speech to parliament), he very kindly took some time out of his busy schedule to attend a training session for what was called "Women in Radio". It was a state sponsored programme to try to get more females employed in "the business", which was notoriously male top-heavy. I was teaching journalism to the 12 young ladies attending the course in Lismore, and wanted to demonstrate how easily they could be manipulated by a politician through insistent rhetoric, a craftily worded press release, and a careful side-stepping of touchy questions. So, what better than to get a real politician in there, hosting a fake news conference. We used all the political banter and flowery adjectives necessary to make the press release a "doozy", and it worked. In the news they produced, they were masterfully manipulated. They learned an important lesson about how to analyse what a politician is saying to you - why it's essential to sit back and think about what they're telling you before dishing it up to the public. I was ever thankful to Charles who played the part perfectly, causing each and every one of my students to fall into the trap.

In more recent times, working in commercial journalism, I see countless examples of press releases that miss the mark, where the actual story is either non-existent or is hidden somewhere towards the end. In all fields in which I have been working in the past few decades, it has to be said the quality is constantly on the slide.

A number of Destination Marketing Organisations representing countries and regions engage people who are no doubt very skilled in destination management, but not so good at putting forward "news" in their own press material. In the field of consumer electronics, even some of the world's biggest manufacturers are capable of turning out utter rubbish. That said, some are very good as well (my hat is off to Ken Hong, former head of global PR for LG Electronics in Seoul, who was exemplary and a reference in the field).

In this section, I am going to quote verbatim some press releases that I feel sorely missed the mark. This in no way is a reflection on the professionalism of the company or organisation for whom they were written, or the quality of their products or services. It can well be a slip-up on the part of the person writing the press release on the day, much like journalists can have bad days on the job.

This said, to be polite, I find that the greater part of press releases that come across the desk "could be better".

When the lead is buried at the end of the story

For the publication ITB Asia News in October 2018, we were sent the following information from the tourism authority of Sabah, Malaysia:

Sabah gives a complete and exotic Bornean experience, from diverse natural offerings such as mountains, islands, beaches, wildlife to warm and hospitable people from various background. It's a combination of fun, adventure and total relaxation in one of the most exciting island State in Malaysia. 20 international cities have regular services to the State capital, Kota Kinabalu. Hong Kong, Shanghai, Tokyo, Singapore, Seoul and business hubs are within short (three to six hours) direct flight and there are easy connections to other long haul destinations. Hotel and resort chains run a vibrant business in Sabah. Joining recently were Hilton Kota Kinabalu and Mercure Kota Kinabalu. This year, Kota Kinabalu Marriot Hotel has joined in the market share in the room division. New high-end resort, Borneo Eagle Resort at Pulau Tiga (where the first reality show Survivor was filmed) is now operational. There are more than 27,000 rooms available in total with around 3,500 rooms in 5-star facilities located throughout the city, coastal areas as well as in the heart of the Bornean rainforest. The top choice Borneo Rainforest Lodge for example, at the Danum Valley Conservation Area is a high-end resort facility located in a virgin rainforest with surroundings hundreds of years of age which includes an ancient burial ground and guaranteed wildlife spotting. In the next 3 years, we will be expecting 11 more hotels ranging from 3 - 5 stars to be opened in Sabah such as Holiday Inn Express, Crowne Plaza Hotel and Pullman. The Sabah International Convention Centre is expected to open in late 2019.

From this, one of our journalists wrote the following article, correcting the one or two spelling errors:

Sabah offers a multitude of opportunities

Sabah gives a complete and exotic Bornean experience, from natural offerings such as mountains, islands, beaches, wildlife to warm and hospitable people from various background.

It's a combination of fun, adventure and total relaxation in one of the most exciting island states in Malaysia. Some 20 international cities have regular services to the state capital, Kota Kinabalu.

Hong Kong, Shanghai, Tokyo, Singapore, Seoul and business hubs are within short (three to six hours) direct flight and there are easy connections to other long-haul destinations.

Hotel and resort chains run a vibrant business in Sabah. Recent openings include Hilton Kota Kinabalu and Mercure Kota Kinabalu. This year, Kota Kinabalu Marriot Hotel has opened.

A new high-end resort, Borneo Eagle Resort at Pulau Tiga (where the first reality show Survivor was filmed) is now operational.

There are more than 27,000 rooms available in total in Sabah, with around 3,500 rooms in five-star facilities located throughout the city, in coastal areas as well as in the heart of the Bornean rainforest.

In the next three years, we will be expecting 11 more hotels ranging from three to five stars to be opened in Sabah such as Holiday Inn Express, Crowne Plaza Hotel and Pullman. The Sabah International Convention Centre is expected to open in late 2019.

...

Given that this was for a NEWS magazine, we **rewrote** the story as follows:

New infrastructure planned for Sabah

With the Sabah International Convention Centre opening its doors in late 2019, 11 new hotels are also set to open in Sabah in the next three years.

The Sabah Tourism Board, present again this year at ITB Asia, has announced that properties such as Holiday Inn Express, Crowne Plaza and Pullman, ranging from three to five stars, are all in the pipeline.

Currently, there are more than 27,000 rooms available in Sabah, with around 3,500 rooms in five-star facilities located throughout the city, in coastal areas as well as in the heart of the Bornean rainforest. Joining recently were Hilton Kota Kinabalu and Mercure Kota Kinabalu.

This year, the Kota Kinabalu Marriott Hotel was opened, and the high-end Borneo Eagle Resort at Pulau Tiga (where the first reality show Survivor was filmed) is now operational. The Borneo Rainforest Lodge also recently opened in the Danum Valley Conservation Area - a virgin rainforest.

Sabah gives a complete and exotic Bornean experience, from natural offerings such as mountains, islands, beaches, wildlife to warm and hospitable people from various background. It's a combination of fun, adventure and total relaxation in one of the most exciting island states in Malaysia.

Some 20 international cities have regular services to the state capital, Kota Kinabalu. Hong Kong, Shanghai, Tokyo, Singapore, Seoul and business hubs are within short (three to six hours) direct flight and there are easy connections to other long-haul destinations.

This was a classic case of "Where's the news?"

The press information sent to us by the Sabah tourism authority was not structured as, or meant to be "news", so it was up to us to look for the news, to make the "story", and to structure the page.

The very last sentence in the original story was in fact our lead. Our journalist no doubt had a bit of jetlag, and "missed the mark". He's actually an excellent journalist and was pretty embarrassed about this afterwards.

Believe me, it happens more often than one might think that good, seasoned journalists, when tired or distracted, or when being expedient with a text, can skip right over the news.

The lessons:

You are the journalist. Read all the way through the information (whether it be a press release, a general info sheet, or other) and find what is the most newsworthy part of it all. In this case, the fact there was a new convention centre about to open up was the news, supported by the fact that this would also be followed by numerous hotel openings.

Bring the story closer to home. We knew the Sabah tourism authority was attending the ITB Asia show. This was pertinent and so I added it to the second paragraph.

Try to extrapolate the key idea in order to make an interesting heading. In this case, what was the story? With all this going on, we could see that it was all about new tourism infrastructure being built. That was the story

...

Trying to figure out what it's actually saying

Here is an example of a press release which, when received, was not used, as we just couldn't figure out what it was about:

Brussels Airport Joins Plug and Play's New Travel & Hospitality Program in Europe

VIENNA, June 18, 2019 /PRNewswire/ -- Brussels Airport announced today its partnership with global innovation platform, Plug and Play. They will work with Plug and Play's newest Travel & Hospitality program in Europe, which is scheduled to officially open in September this year. Brussels Airport joins alongside existing Plug and Play Travel's corporate partners in Europe, including Vienna International Airport, Star Alliance, Swissport, etc.

"We are delighted to announce our innovation partnership with Plug and Play. This partnership is a clear sign of Brussels Airport's ambition to continuously improve and innovate in order to deliver the best services to its clients, passengers and airlines. This will

give us continuous access to the latest developments in all areas of aviation/airport business," explains Arnaud Feist, CEO of Brussels Airport Company.

Plug and Play's Travel & Hospitality program launched in Silicon Valley in 2016 and has expanded to four new locations including Vienna, Abu Dhabi, Shanghai, and Singapore. To this date, the Travel program has 30 corporate partners across sectors such as airports, hotels, online travel agencies, and travel management companies.

Just one issue here... We are at paragraph three, and we still don't actually have any idea <u>what Plug and Play IS</u>. Of course, at the end of the document we find this:

About Plug and Play

Plug and Play is a global innovation platform. Headquartered in Silicon Valley, we have built accelerator programs, corporate innovation services, and an in-house VC to make technological advancement progress faster than ever before. Since inception in 2006, our programs have expanded worldwide to include a presence in over 29 locations globally giving startups the necessary resources to succeed in Silicon Valley and beyond. With over 14,000 startups and 300 official corporate partners, we have created the ultimate startup ecosystem in many industries, including Travel & Hospitality. We currently work with JetBlue Technology Ventures, Carlson Wagonlit Travel, Accor Hotels, AirAsia, Swissport, Star Alliance, Trivago, Delta Air Lines, Changi Airport, TUI Group and many more. We provide active investments with 200 leading Silicon Valley VCs, and host more than 700 networking events per year. Companies in our community have raised over $10 billion in funding, with successful portfolio exits including Danger, Dropbox, Lending Club, and PayPal. For more information, visit www.plugandplaytechcenter.com

Is it just me? What exactly is a "global innovation platform"? Going to their website, we learn that they "connect the best technology start-ups and the world's largest corporations". OK, that sounds a bit more succinct and clear. As it happens, this is quite an important player, and what they are doing is important. Where the press release fails is that it assumes that we all know who they are and what they do right from the very start. But I still can't get my head around what they are doing at an airport.

The lessons:

Never assume your audience knows a lot about your topic (at all);

Use the second paragraph to give background rather than just continuing on;

In the "about" paragraph, use the third person, not the first-person plural (we). In a press statement, unless in a quotation, they should not say "We provide". Instead, it is "They provide". The content of the press release is for publication by media – not in an in-house brochure, or on their website, where they can say "we".

...

Read this and see what's missing...

Winners of 2020 "IMTA Mountain Tourism Awards" Announced
NEWS PROVIDED BY IMTA
Nov 23, 2020, 09:55 ET
GUIYANG, Nov. 23, 2020 /PRNewswire/ -- On November 18, 2020 IMTA Annual Conference was held in Guiyang city of Guizhou province, China, along with a key event – awarding ceremony of 2020 "IMTA Mountain Tourism Awards." Initiated by International Mountain Tourism Alliance (IMTA) and characterized by internationalization, high standard, and innovativeness, the Awards was the first of its kind in the cultural tourism sector.

At the opening ceremony of the Conference, Dominique de Villepin, IMTA Chairman and former Prime Minister of France, delivered a video speech because he could not attend due to the COVID-19 pandemic. He highlighted the significance of mountain tourism innovation, and pointed out that mountain tourism must serve as an advantage for local community development and make greater contributions to the social progress and economic growth. After that, Zhu Shanzhong–Executive Director at the UN World Tourism Organization (UNWTO), Chen Dehai–Secretary-General of ASEAN-China Center, Mahendra Bahadur Pandey--Ambassador of Nepal to China, and many other guests delivered keynote speeches, expressing their expectation on the Conference as well as the promising prospect of mountain tourism.

The competition for the Awards was fierce among cultural tourism enterprises and institution and other mountain destination players this year. The applications of over 100 domestic and overseas projects have been received. Experts in tourism planning, ecological environment, art and culture, and outdoor sport from China, Germany, Korea, France, Switzerland, and the USA participated in the selection.

2020 "IMTA Mountain Tourism Awards" consists of five category awards, namely, Mountain Tourism Sustainable Development Award, Best Mountain Tourism Destination Award, Best Mountain Tourism Outdoor Sport Award, Best Mountain Hiking Route Award, and Best Mountain Tourism Camping Award.

After one and a half months of collection and selection, IMTA announced the 12 winners at the awarding ceremony. Shao Qiwei - IMTA Vice Chairman, Hu Zhongxiong - Vice Governor of the People's Government of Guizhou Province, He Yafei -- IMTA Secretary-General, Xie Jinying -- Director of the Bureau for International Exchange and Cooperation of Ministry of Culture and Tourism of China, and Wei Xiao'an -- President of the 2020 IMTA Mountain Tourism Awards Expert Jury, presented the awards to the winners.

SOURCE IMTA

If, as a journalist, you saw the story and found the header interesting, why might you be a bit frustrated now? Let's not talk about grammatical errors or capitalisation of words that are not proper nouns, or any of the other points that may be underlined.

While declaring that the winners had been announced – the theme of the entire story – no award winners were mentioned at any point. Oops.

The lessons:

Remember to include the key information described in the header;

Pay attention to English usage. Sorry, but it IS important;

If quoting important people, occasionally use actual quotes, rather than paraphrasing.

TRUST, FRIENDSHIP AND INEGRITY

Trust is the basis around which all human relationships revolve. From trust and empathy, friendships evolve. In the business of journalism, the importance of trust and real friendship, along with solid integrity, cannot be overstated, either in building contacts or when doing interviews (the latter may be with people you have just met – but empathy is equally as important).

Often, your job is to try to get information first, or gain information that other people don't have – either for publication, or in building your own knowledge base, without letting the cat out of the bag. Remember, the fact you are a journalist doesn't mean your job is to give out everyone's secrets like a mini version of Wikileaks as soon as you learn something. You may get one or two scoops, but you will soon find yourself becoming very isolated and alone once a few people have had their fingers burned (see more about this in the chapter on "getting screwed"). That's if the information is about them, or could compromise them in some way. On the other hand, if someone who has confidential information that they eventually would like to have leaked – but in the "right" way, comes to like, and they trust you, it is much more likely you will be given the information than someone else. This was the case when, in 1984, I was leaked some information from the state social security authorities in Australia, which resulted in a major exposé and laws being changed (see chapter on "what's news"). At that time, it just so happened that I had become very good friends with someone who knew about the story I was working on, and had a cousin at a very high level in the Federal Government, who managed to get his hands on a copy of the letter that incriminated the state department heads. My friend had to bend over backwards to get the copy of the letter. But she did it for me, as she trusted me, and knew that she was also contributing to an action that could, and in the end, would change many peoples' lives. Thus, the importance of having real friends.

Even if you are simply working on a day-to-day basis with people who may help you with "that little extra" bit of information, take the time to get to know them, in order that they understand you can be trusted. The best way to get people to trust and like you is, of course, to get them to talk about themselves, their work, their families, and so on. As Dale Carnegie once said, *"You can make more friends in two months by becoming interested in other people than you can in two years by trying to get other people interested in you."*

This said, be genuine. Always. Do not try to fake it just so people will help you. It doesn't work like that.

To this end, if you haven't already read Dale Carnegie's "How to Win Friends and Influence People", do yourself a favour and do so. It was written many decades ago, but the lessons are still as true today as they were then.

Avoiding arguments

Another thing Carnegie said, and which can be extremely important in building your contacts and friends, is that the only way to get the best of an argument is to avoid it. Carnegie was echoing the old proverb that *"A man convinced against his will is of the same opinion still".*

Basically, what it means is that if someone you are interviewing, or even just conversing with, says something you know to be totally wrong, you have to be very careful as to how you handle the situation. Telling them simply that they are wrong is the surest way of making an enemy. Showing them why, by Googling information, belittles them and makes them feel bad – even if they appear on the outside not to be. This is even more so when someone is supposed to be an expert in their field, and you catch them out in this way. Part of the problem with this is the fact that it is YOU telling the person they are wrong. One of the remedies to this proposed by Carnegie is not to contradict the person, but to say something like, *"Oh, that's very interesting. It was strange, because I read a report the other day in the Straits Times where they were saying 'XXXXXXX'. I'm sure you must be right though."*

I had a case like this when I was talking to a highly renowned hotel technology consultant – one of the best in the business – and we came to speak about Sharp LCD TVs.

"Oh, Sharp are OK", he said, adding, *"But they don't make their own components. They buy their screens from other companies and just assemble the TVs, putting their badge on them."*

Sharp were in many ways the inventors of LCD TV. And our conversation was in 2010, at a time when Sharp actually did produce their own LCD panels, at factories in Kameyama, Japan (which I had toured), and then at Sakai, where the company was producing the largest LCD "mother glass" of any company – Gen 10, while Samsung were still on Gen 8. I was one of the first western journalists to visit their exceptional state-of-the-art fab near Osaka. I even made several 16-page SPECIALreports for Sharp (custom publishing) on their design and production processes, which were a little different from other manufacturers.

"I think you might find Sharp do actually make their own LCD

panels", I quipped back to my friend.

"No. They don't. They buy it all in and just assemble their sets," he now said in a very assertive tone.

I quickly shut up and changed the subject. I guess he still thinks Sharp don't make their own LCD. In the end, what does it change for me if he does think that? Not much. But it's true that the longing… the itching to correct someone when they are totally off target is very strong. Fight it. Don't do it. You'll keep a lot more friends that way.

Touch me and I'll tell the truth…

Did you know that a simple touch can lead a person to be much more honest with you? Even a total stranger.

As an Aussie, I have to say we are a very tactile people to start with. Australians are always tapping each other on the back or the shoulder. It's part of what we call "mateship". It could also be said that we are very trusting of each other in Oz. That could be a good thing or a bad thing – but it is true. Having, over recent years, heard a number of psychological hypotheses about the connection between touch and trust, I now wonder how much one might have to do with the other in Australia. Probably quite a bit.

This can thus be quite an important factor to keep in mind when interviewing different subjects, as it turns out that touch has an immediate subliminal effect on people – causing them to be more open, more compliant and more honest with you that they would have been otherwise.

Mountains of studies have been undertaken proving a simple touch at the right moment can drastically increase the odds that a request you make will be accepted. While touch simply conveys regard and affection, it can also cause the recipient to feel respect and regard for the person who initiated the touch.

In an experiment, when waitresses were asked to lightly touch a customer on the hand, or on the arm; it was found they would generally receive a larger tip. This happened with both male and female customers even though it did not affect the overall dining experience, or other evaluations given by the individual.

Numerous psychological studies have found that there are tangible changes in peoples' behaviour when they are touched. In the 1980's, researchers undertook a study in which they would leave a coin in a phone booth (remember phone booths?). Then, when a stranger would enter the booth and find the coin, generally putting it in their pocket, the researcher would come back and ask if the person hadn't found a coin. If the researcher touched the stranger on the arm before asking, the stranger would generally always admit they had found a coin, and hand it over. For those who weren't touched, the opposite happened. The stranger, not knowing or caring about the other person, tended more to say that had not found a coin. So touching brings out honesty in people.

In another study in 2010 in France, researchers investigated the effect of touch in the context of selling a second-hand car. A male seller was instructed to slightly touch (or not touch) a man who was interested in the car. After the participant left the seller, a female confederate solicited him, asking him to evaluate the car seller on various dimensions. The results showed that for each dimension that the participants evaluated, the touch condition was associated with statistically higher positive evaluations of the toucher than the no-touch control condition.

When you touch someone, they hardly notice it at all, but major changes happen inside their body. Physical contact releases dopamine, oxytocin, and serotonin in their brain (the "happy" chemicals). At the same time, it lowers their cortisol levels (the stress hormone) which slows their heart rate, reduces feelings of stress, and lessens the fight or flight reaction they may be having. Basically, they relax.

All of this—from a single touch—puts them in the mood to listen, and builds immediate rapport. In the blink of an eye, they are more relaxed and ready to comply instead of annoyed and ready to flee. That is, as long as it is done the right way.

The correct way to use touch

When you ask for something from a stranger, a light touch can be the difference between a cold "no" and a warm "yes." But only if it is done the right way. Everyone can remember having "creepy" people touching them in a way that may have been annoying, inappropriate or upsetting.

The rule for touching someone you don't know well is that it has to be natural, sincere and genuine, generally on the upper arm, and it should be quick and non-descript. In Western culture, the space between the elbow and the shoulder is generally considered the "safe zone." If you don't intimately know the person you're talking to, don't venture outside this zone.

Remember, touch as a tool of persuasion doesn't work if it's noticed. Also, extremely important is eye contact. It must be delivered with a smile. Remember, much of all communication between people is non-verbal, with factors such as posture, facial expression and tone of voice being more important than what you actually say. The line between a welcome and an unwelcome touch is narrow, so be sure to keep it "natural" and "normal".

CONSPIRACIES, PROPAGANDA, THREATS AND MANIPULATION

"Please *listen carefully. I can't talk for long because I think my call may be traced. I think I am being watched and followed"*... When you are a radio journalist and you get a call like this, it is pretty normal to think you have a "nutter" on the other end of the line. I wasn't sure, but it certainly sounded weird. It was in 1980, and I had just been officially graded as a journalist ("D" grade – the starting point), after a number of months of in the field training as a cadet in Canberra. It was mid-afternoon as I was on duty at 2CC newsroom.

"You remember the Commonwealth Heads of Government Meeting bombing at the Hilton Hotel in Sydney?", he said, in a shaky, fast-spoken voice. *"They blamed the Ananda Marga sect. Actually, it was ASIO (eds: the Australian Security Intelligence Organisation). My brother was an ASIO officer, and he designed the bomb. They did it to get more power for phone tapping and stuff, and it all went wrong. They were under a lot of pressure. When my brother said he wanted to come clean, he disappeared. But he gave me the exact design of the bomb. I need to meet you to give you this. If it goes public, I'll be safe. If it doesn't, and they know I have*

this information, I think they'll get me too. I think I'm already being followed."

The bombing of the Sydney Hilton Hotel had happened during the 1978 Commonwealth Heads of Government Meeting (CHOGM). A device hidden in a litter bin exploded, blasting two people to pieces, injuring another fatally and seriously injuring seven others.

My caller asked me to meet him the following day at a set time in front of the miniature submarine next to Canberra's war museum, and said he'd also asked someone from the Canberra Times to come. He promptly hung up. I rang the Canberra Times, and found the journalist he'd spoken to. *"He sounds a bit like a whacko... but who knows? Are you going?"* I asked.

The Canberra Times journalist said yes, he would go, so I said, *"Listen, if you get something, just let me know... no point in two of us wasting our time."*

The next day, I called back, and my fellow journalist had indeed gone to the meeting point, but no one showed. *"It was just another hoax"*, he sighed. *"...a bloody waste of time".*

That episode was placed in the "dim, dark, weird memories" file in my brain, until several years later, when it was exposed by an independent senator who had inside info, that yes, it looked like the bomb had indeed been planted by someone from ASIO. While state inquiries have since been undertaken, a Federal inquiry continues to be refused by the government. I wonder why.

A documentary, entitled "The Hilton Bombing Revisited", written by Daryl Dellora and Ian Wansbrough, screened on the ABC in 1994, has largely exposed what happened, but as no official inquiry has ever been launched, the secret services' dirty little secret will possibly forever remain just that.

The documentary demonstrates that not only has the

question of who bombed the Hilton never been answered, but evidence points to a significant conspiracy involving state and federal government agencies, security and intelligence services and the police, to prevent the identity of the culprits coming to light. Retired senior constable Terry Griffiths, himself terribly mutilated in the blast, is one of the key witnesses. The core of the documentary is the contention by Griffiths that the Hilton carnage was the result of a coordinated operation by ASIO, the army and the NSW Special Branch.

Now my nutter on the phone takes on a whole new light. When this guy called me, none of this was out in the open. There was perhaps only one way he could have had that information. It was possible that yes, his brother had designed and built the bomb, and yes, he and his brother may well have been snuffed to avoid collateral damage.

It turns out that on the night of the Hilton bombing, the plan was for a bomb warning to be made, for the police department to be officially alerted and for the area to be evacuated. The military bomb disposal unit was to come with its remote robot and explode the bomb in front of the world's media.

The motive was to secure greater powers for ASIO and to deflect increasing criticism of, and political opposition to ASIO and the state police special branches. The plan went terribly wrong when a garbage truck came by 20 minutes earlier than usual. While a warning call was received at police HQ, it was not passed on and the police on duty did not prevent the bomb being placed in the garbage compactor and detonated.

The lessons: Keep an open mind. Don't be naïve and swallow everything, but do understand that the highest powers in each nation do have secret agendas, propagate propaganda to their own benefit, and lie to the public and the media. The secret services are not above either setting-up a dastardly act or at least turning a blind eye to one if it means getting what they want in the longer term.

What's the agenda?

The Watergate scandal of course was probably one of the bigger scoops when it came to corruption at the highest level. More recently, of course, there was 9/11 where it appears possible that the US secret services may well have sat back and let it happen. So, what was the "agenda" of the US Government? As usual, money and power. The hysteria that was engendered by these horrific acts of terrorism allowed the US to tag pretty well anyone wearing a turban and as "one of them". Despite the fact the 9/11 terrorists primarily came from Saudi Arabia, no action of any kind was recommended against Saudi Arabia. Why? Because the Saudi government holds large quantities of US bonds as a means of lending money to the USA. If they were to become pissed off for any reason and cash-in the bonds, they could cause major damage to the US economy. Instead, the US (and the UK) had their eyes on the oil in the gulf that used to be theirs – controlled by Iraq. While Iraq had absolutely no involvement of any kind with 9/11, the US reacted to the 9/11 attacks not only by hitting Afghanistan, but in particular by invading Iraq. The "terrorism hysteria" worked wonders in terms of softening opposition to the invasion of Iraq.

I was in a bar near Dallas, Texas when a newsflash came on the TV announcing that the US was going into Iraq, and a couple of locals asked me what I thought about it. *"We're gonna go in there and whip the ass of that damned terrorist dictator"*, they said, obviously well versed from what they had been force-fed by the US mass media, who were, in turn, repeating everything they were being told by the administration. What else could they do?

"You're an Aussie… you guys are on our side. But you live in France? The French have got no backbone… No guts… They're not going in… They are chicken shit," they said.

I replied, *"It's all about the oil".*

"Huh?", they retorted. *"Of course not. Saddam's a terrorist. He's got the bomb. If we don't go in now, he'll use it."*

I had to work hard not to poke too much fun at them. Remember I was a lone Aussie in a big bar full of sweaty men wearing Stetsons, broidered shirts and fancy riding boots (some with spurs). Texas redneck cowboys quite like Aussies... as long as the Aussies don't take them for idiots. Which I certainly wasn't going to do. They were only repeating the sole information with which they had been indoctrinated and which they believed implicitly.

"You know the French oil company Elf signed some big contracts with the authorities in Iraq," I suggested. *"It would seem pretty strange that the French would go and kick the arse of someone with whom they just signed a major economic agreement, wouldn't it?"*

They looked puzzled. It could have been because I said, *"with whom"*, but I think it was more like a little glimmer of light going off in their brains that they were not used to having, that maybe something might have been kept from them.

In the end, of course, Saddam didn't have the bomb, and the US and its allies took back control of the oil, much to the dismay of the French who had been so secretly proud of the deal Elf had done behind the scenes not so long before. Claiming to go in and help the Iraqi people, it is very clear that the US forces did the total opposite, freeing the country up for the arrival of Isis, and turning much of it into a hell-hole. But that's OK. They got the "precioussssss" oil.

Should one interview dictators?

I often wondered what Saddam was really like as a person. I almost had the chance to find out in 2001. In April of that year I received a call from Catherine Colona de Stigliano, an Italian Princess who organised the "Bal de l'été" (Summer Ball) in Monaco, whom I had known for some time, having interviewed her for radio and TV. She knew I had been doing quite a bit of work over the past year with a supermodel who was regularly in the press as she had been frequenting Prince Albert of Monaco on a regular basis. Catherine told me she had a mission on which she would like to invite her.

"Another Princess and myself have teamed together with Sophie Audouin-Mamikonian of Armenia," she said. *"A member of the Royal family of Jordan is lending her a 747 jet, a pharmaceutical company in Switzerland is donating a large quantity of medical supplies, and we are going to Iraq to deliver them directly to a hospital in Baghdad, to ensure they really get to where they are supposed to go."*

There had been a blockade on the shipment of pretty well anything to Iraq, and it had been said that medical supplies would simply go to the military; not to the public. But three Princesses delivering the supplies direct to the hospital... That could work.

The supermodel's manager considered the risk factor outweighed the benefit of her joining the fray.

"Why don't you come with us anyway as media and cover the event?", suggested Catherine.

I jumped at the opportunity, and Catherine sent me the itinerary by fax on my new-fangled Nokia 9110 phone (remember faxes?). It went something like this: *"Flight arrives at Baghdad airport, motorcade with military escort to the hotel; the entire hotel will be booked for this occasion. Meeting with President. Travel with ground transport to hospital for delivery of medical supplies. Official dinner."* ... So it went on.

I called Catherine. *"Which President are they talking about? The President of the hospital?"*

"No... Saddam." she said.

I was gobsmacked. I was going along on a mission where we were going to meet the man who was, at that time, the world's most notorious dictator.

"Do you think I can get an interview?"

"Yes. There is going to be a press conference with the local media. You will be the only one from the west."

I didn't like that. If everyone gets the same Q&A, there is little value in the story. I had to think fast, and came up with a crazy idea, as I had heard there was a problem finding someone to pay for the fuel for the flight. *"If I guarantee to pay for the fuel for your 747... all of it... do you think you can organise an exclusive – one on one – interview?"*

The fuel was going to cost a lot. It was, after all, a 747, running a full load. But having contacted Sipa Press in Paris and my European contact for CNN, I was assured that if I indeed did get an exclusive interview in video and print, it would be worth a hell of a lot more than a full tank for a 747.

A few days later, Catherine got back to me and said Saddam had agreed to the interview. I didn't talk about it with too many people. But of those who did know, a number said to me, *"How can you interview a dictator? You shouldn't be promoting him."*

This created a new point of perspective. Would I, by interviewing Saddam, be "promoting" him? Would that be a bad thing? Should a dictator be able to say, in public, what he wants / thinks, even though it was often apparent he was lying? What effect would this have on the world? Or on the public at large?

To me, the bigger questions included whether my interview with Saddam would influence or affect the way the west was working on painting him into a corner. Could I be partially screwing up their plans? Even a little bit? What might that mean?

What was the danger? I realised that if I was under a personal threat of any kind, it would not be from someone on the Iraqi side, but from "our" side.

In my very early days as a journalist, I came to understand that our job was to give equal say to both sides on any argument, whether political or other, and that the listeners / readers / viewers were thus able to decide for themselves.

This began to change largely in the USA under the Reagan administration in 1987, when what was known as the Fairness Doctrine was abolished. Introduced by the US Federal Communications Commission in 1949, this was a law that put the onus on broadcasters to present controversial issues in a manner deemed to be honest, equitable and balanced. The doctrine didn't necessarily require equal time on all sides, but required that contrasting viewpoints be presented. It didn't apply to newspapers, as in theory any number of competing publications were allowed, thus supposedly giving balance in that way.

In a utopian world where journalists actually work as journalists, my hope is still that balance should be given. In any case, it must be our aim.

When interviewing Saddam, even if I asked questions that may have put him on the spot, he would have answered with whatever rhetoric he felt like. Probably a lot of lies, but in any case, it would be his point of view. Today, one might ask how this might be different to an interview with Donald Trump.

The flight was planned for July 2001. Not long before the departure date we were informed that there was a cholera outbreak in Baghdad and that the mission was pushed back to the end of September. On the September 11, our plans to go to Baghdad were set aside, as, in the following days, George W. Bush decided the best way to correct the wrongs of a bunch of

Saudis flying planes into strategic targets in the US was to invade Afghanistan and then, less than two years later, Iraq. As Randy Newman may well have said, "Boom goes Baghdad".

The rot sets in

It must be said that over the past twenty or so years, the rot has been setting in when it comes to the political or corporate manipulation of mainstream news. In his excellent book "Rather Outspoken: My Life in the News", Dan Rather reveals, in detail, his behind the scenes view of CBS News as part of the big CBS corporate machine. Rather was, for many decades, the "face" of what was no doubt the most highly respected broadcast news service in the USA, and of which United Network Radio News in Australia was an affiliate when I was working there in the 1980s.

He talks about when, for him, the rot started to set in. It was in 2004. During the war in Iraq , personnel of the US Army and the CIA committed a series of human rights violations against detainees in the Abu Ghraib prison in Iraq. These violations included physical and sexual abuse, torture, rape, sodomy, and murder. The abuses came to public attention with the publication of photographs of the abuse by CBS News in April 2004. The incidents received widespread condemnation both within the United States and abroad, although the soldiers received support from some conservative media within the United States.

The administration of George W. Bush asserted that the abuses at Abu Ghraib were isolated incidents and were not indicative of US policy. This assertion was disputed by humanitarian organisations such as the Red Cross, Amnesty International, and Human Rights Watch. These organisations stated that the abuses at Abu Ghraib were part of a wider pattern of torture and brutal treatment at American overseas detention centres, including those in Iraq, in Afghanistan, and at Guantanamo Bay. In outlining the difficulties in getting the

Abu Graib story on air, Rather unveiled the gory details of internal workings at a high corporate level of the company.

"The relationship between government and the media and the large corporations that own the media, will always be complex, in part because media giants will always need something from government – licence renewals, permission to expand, and so forth," said Rather.

A symbiotic relationship between media and government does not serve the public well, explains Rather: *"When I say that big business is in bed with big government it is for their mutual benefit, not for the benefit of the public interest."*

Rather says the possibility that the financial and political interests of CBS Corporate almost buried a story as compelling as Abu Graib was most unsettling, adding, *"Little did I know that it was only going to get worse from there. Much worse."*

Wikileaks – a hard one to call

The way I understand it, Julian Assange one day came upon a cool idea, wherein he could uncover all kinds of dirt through his wiki site, and it would be a good thing for the world, and he could become famous in the process.

Wikileaks did uncover some incredible shit as an open platform where insiders who had bad stuff to leak could do so with relative impunity. Thus, among the many revelations, we witnessed the so-called "Collateral Murder" video in 2010, a classified video from the US military which showed the murder of a number of people in a town in Iraq by US soldiers, including two employees of the news agency Reuters. The helicopter crew simply mowed-down a group of unarmed people in an open square. Then a van drove up to save the wounded. The driver had two children with him. You could hear the soldiers say: *"Well it's their fault for bringing their kids into a battle"*. And then they open fire. The father and the wounded were immediately killed, while the children survived with serious wounds.

Through the publication of that video, the world became a direct witness to a terrible criminal massacre.

By uncovering this kind of horror, Wikileaks created a huge amount of embarrassment for the US military establishment. Not so much because it happened, but because it happened with impunity. We learned that today, just like in many other conflicts in the past, war crimes could be committed with total impunity. Those who did this would not even be cited by their superiors.

This embarrassment caused the CIA to react, and to trump-up crimes against Assange (pardon the pun) in order to get him out of the way.

At the same time, in the run-up to the 2016 US elections, Wikileaks uncovered thousands of Hilary Clinton's emails that turned out to be very damaging, and were highly instrumental in helping Donald Trump get into power. Over 50,000 pages of documents spanning from 2010 to 2014 were revealed. We are told this was done because they "could" do it. But then why not uncover Trump's tax statements? Why only hit one side, with such terrible collateral damage? Just because they "could"? Sorry, I don't believe that.

So how was Assange manipulated? Was he so naïve that he believed there could be no manipulation, and that the modern concept of propaganda belonged to the cold war era?

No. Someone else was quick to figure out where the crack was in Assange's system, and leverage it. Believing that the end consumer of information would be smart enough in every instance to be able to decide upon the validity and the kind of news by which they might be influenced is utopian to the Nth degree. They're not. They never have been.

We never have been. That's why propaganda works, and why, as governments and their cronies realise they can increasingly manipulate information thanks to the onset of the digital age, we have a much bigger role to play in terms of vetting and verifying information, and its pertinence to the world.

It's also why balance is ESSENTIAL, not optional.

That's where, for me, Assange's model screwed up. He was shooting in the dark. He was brave and clever for having uncovered some terrible shit. But I believe he made a big mistake in not weighing up the power he possessed and how he should use it.

What would it have cost him to sit on the Hilary "scum" story until after the elections? Bad call, mate.

When should you give up?

The image of the hardened journalist battling to get the facts at any cost is a great cliché. Indeed, many are those who lose their lives in the line of duty as war reporters, and some get snuffed for getting "too close to the flame" in affairs of major corruption. I have never been in a position where my life was threatened directly. But I've seen it first-hand.

In 1987, living in Ventimiglia on the Italian Riviera when I was working at what was then Riviera 104 in nearby Camporosso Mare, every weekend saw us, along with a motley bunch of ex-pat radio people and journalists, at the same mythical bar called Bananarama. Bananarama was known primarily for four things: very cheap drinks, great ambiance, trendy music, and Anna. Anna was the waitress and girlfriend of Sergio, the jovial, chubby, bearded owner of the establishment. Countless females from surrounding districts who came to the bar did their utmost to look like Anna. They tried particularly hard to copy the elegance and style of this – always dressed in black – local idol. None quite succeeded at the task.

One Saturday, I was at the bar with Andrew Astbury, a young radio presenter whose dad had also been programme director at Riviera 104, before the station moved to Monaco and changed its name to Riviera Radio. Andrew and I were, as one is wont to do at bars like this late in the evening, having an Indian arm-wrestle. As this was happening, a (very) heavily-built Italian came alongside us, and said *"I'll play the winner"*. As it turned out it was me, but I told him that as he was much bigger than me, it was going to be an easy win for him.

"Never mind", he said, *"I will buy you a drink anyway"*.

He beat me, of course, and bought Andrew and me a beer, and then another one. He told us he lived near the rustic mediaeval village of Dolceacqua up in the hills, where he had a small vineyard. Anna occasionally darted worried looks at me as she served the drinks. Towards the end of the evening, someone walking past our table spilt the remnants of our host's drink. The perpetrator hurried to the bar, bought another drink, and brought it back to our table, trembling. On our way out later, I asked Sergio who this guy really was that we were drinking with.

"He is the heat man", he said.

It took a moment for it to sink in.

He repeated. *"He is heat man for la famiglia. You should be careful."*

From what I learned later, the "heat" (hit) man had been freed from prison not long before this. The way it worked was that local newspapers would run a nice story on a mafia guy being put in jail, then – on a technical hitch – he would be let out not too long afterwards. I really can't confirm if it really happened like that, but that's what I was told.

A few months later a UK journalist friend, Neil Marr, was working in the area and had moved into a small village house in Dolceacqua. He was producing a series of articles for the UK press on the mafia, and how it was infiltrating into the UK. As it turned out, a number of local bosses were based between Ventimiglia and San Remo, and their operatives were based in Camporosso, between our radio offices and the village of Dolceacqua. Neil's choice of where to live obviously left something to be desired. He had already filed some stories when one evening, after crossing the pedestrian bridge to enter the village, he was mugged, with a warning to leave town... or face a much worse fate.

He didn't leave town.

The result was that a week or so later, upon arriving home one night, when he opened the door, his house exploded. A gas bottle had been placed inside the door, ready to go off at his arrival. Scattered on the path outside were scrunched-up pages from UK dailies. His articles. The message couldn't have been clearer.

Neil didn't die in the explosion (he sadly has since, however, from less violent causes). He took the full force of the blast and received third degree burns to a good part of his body. He was so badly burned that he had to be flown to the UK for specialist treatment and skin grafts, and spent months in hospital.

It was most likely our "friend" from the bar who perpetrated the act. Indeed, for Neil, it was time to give up – on that one.

Neil never went back to that part of Italy. He went on to create, with his younger brother Alec (sadly also departed), a successful media agency on the French Riviera, doing glitz and glamour feature stories for the UK press. It turns out movie stars and royalty are much less likely to want to kill you.

The lessons:

Listen to your gut instinct.

Keep an open mind at all times. Conspiracy does happen.

Not all the time, but probably more than one might like to believe. Don't be naïve, and believe that corruption, collusion manipulation and conspiracy belong to the past. They are growing in importance as time goes on, as those in power have learned how to better influence a greater part of the mass media, keeping those who try to run real news "under control" via smoke screens and blockading.

ALL governments have political agendas that are kept secret from the greater public. This has always been the case. It's not new. The reasons for the secrets however differ greatly, and the degrees of corruption of course vary as well. Many have written on this topic, and we continue to discover, almost always with stupor, the depths to which state security forces and politicians are able to descend to protect their own interests, rather than the interests of the nation at large – or the people. When it comes to declaring war, this is even more evident.

Do NOT be led into believing that *everything* comes down to conspiracies. It doesn't. Be cynical, but be discerning and try to analyse all aspects of the information you are obtaining.

Corrupt people (and organisations) can be extremely dangerous. Keep it in mind.

GETTING SCREWED

While getting screwed litterally might be very pleasant, in work, as a journalist, it's not, and I say this through solid experience. It would be difficult to give enough emphasis to the importance of avoiding this fate when possible. Sounds obvious, but if you are ever working freelance for a major agency, beware. The bigger the job you land, the bigger the chances there will be hyenas hovering around waiting to snap at your work with no concern whatsoever for your reputation.

Probably the best case I can remember, and there were a few, was in 1999. I had done a couple of jobs for Sipa – a big French photo/press agency, working alongside top-line photographers on the editorial side of the projects. They called me with a new idea.

"We have an award-winning German photographer who's keen to do a glamour shoot with the wives and girlfriends of Formula One drivers. Do you want to work on the project with her?"

Of course, I did, and after some discussion, we came up with the idea of donating a major percentage of the proceeds from the magazine sales to charity – something that made the shoot more attractive to the subjects.

It was a long and convoluted process, going through drivers' agents, and finally settling on days and times for the work to be done. After the photographer did the super glamour black & white photos, I would interview each of the ladies. In the end, we had sessions with Erja Hakkinen, Corinna Schumacher, and girlfriends of David Coulthard and Heinz-Harald Frentzen. Rather than do a straight up and down interview, I thought it would be interesting to have five "key" words: *"power, passion, love, speed and fear"*; and to get each lady to talk about each concept and what it meant to her, of course in the context of her relationship with the driver. Then, rather than present each interview one after the other, each key word would be followed by their statements. Everyone thought the idea was good, and the discussions were quite enthralling.

In passing, I spoke about the project to a German TV producer I knew who was based in the south of France, and he asked if he could video the photo shoots if he promised the footage would only be screened after the magazines were published – as a promotion for the articles, to which everyone agreed.

I was about to learn a lesson about naivety, and stupid, blind trust.

It's the job of the photo/press agency to present the work to a broad range of magazines around the world and to negotiate the best price and conditions. Once we'd finished the photo shoots and I'd written up the texts, several big-name magazines said they were very interested in buying. We learned that a famous German magazine was going to run with the story (having two German drivers' "other halves", that seemed normal).

That's when the bomb hit. I received a call from one of the driver's agents. *"A TV report has just gone out in Germany with some very unflattering angles of the girls in the photo shoots. What the fuck is going on?"*

What? I had been assured by my "friend" that the TV report would be kosher, and not only that, it would go out only after the magazine article was published; not before. I called him and he assured me that the channel was not supposed to run with it… a number of excuses that sounded plausible, but which didn't get around the fact that he had no doubt been paid very handsomely for having passed on the video images before the magazines hit the stands. Whatever the story was, the girls, their husbands and their agents were very pissed off. So were the editors of the German magazine who, while still running the story, had been pipped to the post.

The next week, I was still seething and kicking myself when I got a call from the agency. It was excellent news. The hugely successful French magazine Paris Match had bought the rights to the story, and paid very well. Wow. At least there was a little justice in the world, or so I thought. I couldn't wait to pick up the magazine the following week at the news agents.

The story was there alright; but not as I had written it. The title was "Celles qui ont épousée la peur" (*Those who married fear*). As it turned out, the previous weekend, there had been a horrific accident during the Formula One race at Spa Francorchamps involving David Coulthard, who escaped miraculously. The magazine editors decided to run only the statements about **fear**, as if that was the only thing the girls had spoken about.

I received another call from Hakkinen's manager. *"You've screwed us with this story."* I tried to tell him that no, I was the screwee, not the screwer, but he wouldn't hear anything of it. In fact, he was right. They HAD been screwed and it WAS by my stupidity in not overseeing what was going on, not having a better handle on it, and not having detailed agreements with everyone involved.

I should have learned from an earlier experience with the same German TV "friend". He had offered me a large sum of cash in 1997 when I was working for a company working in the field of Formula One. I had been asked by a TV production company in Monaco working for Williams to transcribe radio conversations between that year's world champion, Jacques

Villeneuve and his pit crew on the last race in Jerez, Spain, as they were difficult to understand at times, and they felt I had a "good ear".

It was there, where following a tangle between Villeneuve and Michael Schumacher a few laps from the end of the race, Mika Hakkinen and David Coulthard were right behind Villeneuve as he nursed his car, concerned that some damage might put him out of the race before crossing the finish line. All he needed was one point to win the championship. In the end, Hakkinen and Coulthard slipped past in the last moments, and, by coming in third, Villeneuve won the championship.

I was privy to all that went on between Villeneuve and his pit crew. And I can say today that more was said than what has since been released in an online audio clip. By respect for the people I was working for, I did not reveal publicly what was said, and would not do so even today. At the time, when I told the German producer I was working on the tape, he offered me a very tidy sum for me to "leak" him a copy. The cash would have come very much in handy at that time, but the answer was no.

"No one will ever know where it came from", he said. Oh yeah? How many people are working with tapes of that stuff? Get real. Of course, they would have figured it out, and I would be screwed. Of course, he would have made many times what he was willing to give me if he had sold the recording. That's all he was concerned about. So, two years later, why did I trust him to work on the Formula One wives story? Christ knows. And even there, I'm not so sure.

TOOLS OF THE TRADE

A poor tradesman blames his tools. The adage also goes for those working in the media. Being sure of your equipment sounds like a basic premise, but it's not always that easy. In this section, I'll give you a few useful anecdotes, and one or two tips.

As you will remember, I started out my career working in radio in Australia. As a news journalist in the 1980s, we would generally use Marantz Superscope cassette recorders for interviews, or, in cases where quality needed to be even higher (i.e. for a documentary report) we'd use a Uher reel-to-reel (quarter inch) recorder. From the former, the tape would be loaded onto another reel-to-reel tape machine in the newsroom, from which we would generally "drop edit". This entailed "dropping" selected sound bites from one tape to another – in sequence – to create the final result desired. We would then dub the final result onto a "cart" – or cartridge – which was a ready-to-play quarter-inch tape that automatically queued itself at the start – ready to go. The cartridges looked the same as the 8-tracks that made an appearance in the 1970s primarily for car audio. In the news booth, we thus had two or more cart machines that would play our news grabs (and in the main on-air studio, all ads were also played from cart). It also meant several generations of analogue audio, with each one losing quality.

Oh, you who were born into the digital age, little do you know of the difficulties of analogue editing. This could also entail splicing: the physical cutting and sticky-taping reel-to-reel tape – generally on a big Revox machine – to get your desired result. Doing this on tape that had already been spliced often meant audio drops, tape sticking to the drive-wheel, and lots of other fun stuff. We also occasionally worked with four or eight track analogue recorders that were relatively commonplace in bigger radio stations as they were also used for making ads.

Operating remotely, we were given some interesting bits of kit, including a cable – equipped on one end with a jack fitting the output port of the cassette recorder – and the other end equipped with two tiny alligator clips. At the time, of course, there were no mobile phones, and the only way to communicate with the office was via the two-way radio in our cars, or via a public phone. To send audio, one had simply to call the office via any landline – generally in these cases, phone booths. They would patch a tape recorder at the other end, and then it was time to plug in the "magic cable". For this, one would unscrew the mouthpiece of the phone, attach the two alligator clips to the now exposed phone wires, and press the "play" button.

My first revelation that things don't always go to plan happened one fine day in Sydney, when I had been sent out by radio 2UE to cover a "closed-door" meeting between a group of employers and a union, trying to beat out a solution to a strike that had been plaguing the city for some time. Along with a number of other TV, radio and print reporters, I was waiting on the steps of the arbitration commission, when the union leader came out to make his statement. A bunch of microphones were thrust under his nose – including mine – as he made his all-important statement about the end of the strike.

I should probably underline the fact at this point that at this time, 2UE was number one in Sydney, and we had the biggest network of stations across the state taking our news. They were counting on me to get the story as it happened, and to get it right.

With 25 minutes to spare before the top of the hour, I knew I could send the audio comfortably. What I didn't count on was the fact that with my recorder over my shoulder, one of my competitors had unbeknown to me unplugged my microphone jack from my recorder. When I listened back, I had no audio at all. Just "shhhhhhhhhh". And for me, it was just "shhhhhhhhhhiiiit"!

Here, I learned (very quickly) another lesson. I had always wondered why the bag they gave me to go and record interviews had so many different leads and jacks. Thankfully, also present at the meeting, there was a camera crew from our TV partner station, Channel 9. I ran over and asked them if I could get a dub of the audio from their camera to my machine – as I thankfully had the right jack (big cannon to small). A few minutes later, I had the audio, and I sent it to the station. They were able to break the news at the top of the hour, and I didn't end up getting my arse kicked. No-one back at the station had any idea what had happened. Thankfully, or I would have been a laughing stock.

Lesson

In the end, the lesson was "Don't necessarily trust people from competing media. Keep a closer eye on your gear, and be bloody thankful to have people there that have your back."

Fast forward to France and my post-radio days. Working in print, I have always been an advocate of recording interviews, not just taking notes (see the section on interviews). In 1997, a "big" one was for Sipa press. A full day with Prince Albert of Monaco, on the occasion of the 700th anniversary of the arrival of the Grimaldi Family in the Principality... doing photos and a long interview. As Princess Diana had died the week before the interview (which had been programmed long before), this added a lot of interest for foreign media. Princess Grace had been iconic in her time, and, amongst other things, I asked Prince Albert what advice he could give to Diana's sons, having been very much in the same position decades before. The entire interview was recorded with my then new minidisc recorder. But to be safe, I also recorded with my old Sony Walkman cassette recorder. Lucky, as the minidisc shut down after ten minutes, leaving only the old faithful Sony to finish the job. Imagine the catastrophe if, after getting the prince to talk for around an hour, the recording had failed. I don't think he would have been very keen to start again.

Indeed, the minidisc, while having good audio quality, was not so reliable. Apparently not having learnt from my lessons of the past, in 1999, I occasionally used a minidisc recorder when working alongside German photographer Vanessa Von Zitzewitz, on the book "Monachrome". One interviewee was Luciano Pavarotti. We met with him at the Salle Garnier in Monaco – backstage at the opera house. He only had a few minutes, and I knew it. As the minidisc recorder took almost a minute to boot up, I had already started the machine ready to record, and had just to hit the pause button again for it to record. When Pavarotti was ready, I hit the button... and the whole thing shut down. Boom! He looked at me as if I was an idiot, as if to say, *"What kind of journalist comes to interview me... the great Pavarotti... and screws up like this?"*

Well, I guess an Aussie who had too much faith in his minidisc recorder.

It took me around a minute to start the recording process again, with this sweaty, angry, bearded opera icon frowning at me from his deep red and gold throne-like chair, under what appeared to be bushier eyebrows than usual. Strike that: Yes, he correctly guessed I was an idiot – as I was that day. Sometimes, we all can be. But in the end, the interview was fine, and the content of the book was not compromised.

Dictating to Siri

As time goes on, the demands to process information faster and faster increase exponentially. One of the most tedious tasks for any journalist is that of transcribing a long interview. Occasionally we had looked at using transcription services, which is a clumsy way of doing it, because they write the text verbatim, and occasionally misinterpret what was said. In the past couple of years, however, the arrival of Siri and other such personal assistants has provided a solution. In fact, we began using this system when working to very tight TV deadlines for motorsports shows, where transcriptions of the interviews were required as part of the script, so that they could then be quickly translated and dubbed into other languages on stations such as Eurosport.

This is how it's done: It's best to use noise-cancelling headphones, through which you listen back to the interview. On your phone, create a note, and dictate the text as you are listening to it. This enables you to speak clearly – so the voice recognition works efficiently, and also means you can omit parts you want to omit, or change phraseology where necessary.

In this way, an interview that may be half an hour long can be transcribed and edited live in much less than an hour. If the phone and your PC are connected via the cloud (i.e., iCloud), the note will automatically appear on your PC (or Mac). If you do manage to speak clearly, you won't need to do much correcting. It can be a great time saver. No doubt, in the years following the publication of this work, the technology will evolve to the point where the result will be virtually flawless.

Online transcription services such as Amberscript are now also very useful - as long as the accent of the interviewee is not too strong.

Other online tools

Other useful online tools include OCR – optical character

recognition – for when you have a large amount of text to transcribe from a printed page or an image file.

For translation, I tend to use Reverso translator, which is getting better all the time.

SOCIAL LEVEL

At a company level, it is very easy to place people because of their title. In different cultures, there are different levels of snobbism between these social levels, and in all cultures, there are some people for whom social level is important. Interestingly, the title of "journalist", "editor", "analyst", or "editor in chief" – even if it's for quite a small group, puts you in a "hazy" zone, where people can't really peg you on the social scale.

This can sometimes be a great thing, especially in places like Japan, where the fact that company vice-presidents can only frequent others at the same level within their own company. This can make life for them a little tedious. You thus have the possibility to make great contacts at a high level, as these people seek ways to escape the drudgery of their daily lives.

On the other hand, in other cultures, like the UK, being labelled as a journalist is not a plus. I have seen this at different levels. It is particularly the case with rich snobs, who can be particularly acrimonious when they are faced with "the press". I discovered this after having given a hand, for a number of years, to my friends John Martinotti and Melissa Corken, the organisers of the World Music Awards in Monaco (and in Las Vegas, Los Angeles and London). Over more than 20 years, I coordinated media activities for them, organising press conferences for the "stars", writing press releases, and basically making sure the media attending the event got what they wanted.

One evening, a number of years back, we were invited, with the artists, for a soirée on a yacht belonging to a very well-known UK billionaire who was a sponsor of the show. I had met his wife a few times before, and found her to be charming and very open. On that evening, our man was welcoming the people on his yacht, when he introduced himself to me, and asked what I did. *"I work with the press for the World Music Awards... I'm the media guy."*

Quite obviously not the thing to announce to him that night. *"Oh. Media... Hmmmphf"*, he sneered and grunted, turning his back on me and talking to worthier (and potentially more useful) people.

I figure that for him at that time, a "media guy" was basically the equivalent to being a worthless piece of crap, as I was neither a top model, nor a "money" guy... so just a piece of insignificant rubbish. I think the right word might be "contempt".

Not everyone is like that, however. I have been able to develop very cordial and friendly relations with Government Ministers, rock stars and even Albert II, the Sovereign Prince of Monaco. This comes through the fact that these people just happen to be nice, and unaffected by their position.

I have a theory. I reckon that people who grow up being normal, nice, simple (in the good sense) and unaffected, remain that way when they become rich and famous – or even just famous. People who have a chip on their shoulder, who are arrogant, snide, belittling or aloof, have these traits magnified when they become famous. In this sense, arseholes become very big arseholes when they're famous. In any case it's my theory, and I've seen a big enough bunch of famous arseholes; but I've also seen many nice, normal, humble, friendly people in the same position (i.e. singers such as Jennifer Lopez, The Bee Gees, Olivia Newton John, Shirley Bassey, Tony Hadley, Morten Harket (A-Ha), Jennifer Paige; or the likes of supermodel Claudia

Schiffer, writer Kurt Vonnegut, or actors such as Roger Moore, Sharon Stone, Kevin Costner, Robert Wagner ... the list goes on...). All nice, normal and unaffected – at least when I saw them.

Let me give you an example on the "nice" side. It was when I was doing my magazine show, Sunday, on TMC in Monaco. This particular week, I had been told Shirley Bassey was to give a concert in Monaco at the Sporting Club – a prestigious venue on the eastern end of the Principality. The organisers had let me know Shirley would be willing to do an interview at the club just before her rehearsals on the Thursday afternoon – the day before her show. I thus planned to make that the main part of my half-hour show. I was waiting with my camera crew – who had set up an interview spot behind the club looking out over the sea – as Shirley turned up for the rehearsals quite late, due to the traffic coming over from Nice.

I introduced myself and said we were there for the interview, but with time being short, she said she didn't think it would be possible any more. I explained however that "she was it" for my show, and that the camera was set up and ready to go. She agreed and came out on the terrace where we had a very interesting chat. I remember one of the things that really puzzled me was, *"How, after singing 'Goldfinger', or 'Hey, Big Spender' literally thousands of times in front of different publics, could you keep doing it without getting bored?"*

"I look into the eyes of the people standing in front of the stage," she said. *"For them, for many of them, this is the first time they may have seen me singing these songs live. That's why they are here. And so, for me, every time is like the first time when I look into their eyes."*

It was a great interview. I was very happy. Then the head technician came over and said to Shirley, *"Everything is set up. We already have all your microphone settings. We're all good. You don't need to do a run through."* To which Shirley said, *"OK",* and prepared to leave.

"*Oh...*" I said.

"*Is there a problem?*" Shirley asked.

"*Errrr... It's just that to illustrate the report, we really wanted to get some images of you singing during the rehearsals. So, if you don't, we miss out.*"

Shirley smiled. "*That's okay. I can sing something for you. Now I have the time.*"

My cameraman and assistant took their positions in the middle of the empty hall, as Shirley climbed onto the stage. She sang two songs along with the orchestra, just for us. Just for my programme. She had no need to do that in terms of "promotion", as her show was already sold out. It was just through professional conscience and just plain niceness that she did it. She created a magical moment, and I am sure the people who watched that report on my show the next Sunday felt the magic. They must have felt the goodness of her soul. I am sure of that.

People talk about Karma, and I don't know how it works, but I do believe it works. On every level of society. With every kind of person. Here is one way it works. I am talking about that moment right now. It wasn't isolated. I've had many, many moments when very famous people have gone the extra mile to be nice and to help. I could fill up a book with them. Maybe that will be a next edition.

A FEW MORE TIPS

Here are a few (assorted) tips to keep in mind that will be useful in keeping you ahead of the game, or in getting you there.

Have a genuine interest in people and things...

It is absolutely vital to your work that you have a real, genuine interest in the people you talk to, and what they have to say. Sometimes, the topics you may be sent to cover may not, at the outset, seem to be enthralling. But it's up to you to make the best of what you have.

If you find a topic or a person boring, it is possibly because you have not taken the time to really interest yourself in it, or them. You will find that if you put some time and effort into aspects of topics that bore you, digging a little deeper, you will find something interesting. It is even possible that you will find quite a few interesting things if you look hard enough. Sometimes you really have to dig, but you will eventually find something. In fact, you will find there are no dull people or topics when you make an intentional effort to find out what might make them interesting. This will help you enormously when it comes to your work, and will make you feel better about life in general.

I learned this when I was still 19, working as a presenter on radio 2LF in the town of Young, New South Wales (my first full-time on-air job). I was doing the afternoon shift, from

2pm 'till 6pm. On Wednesdays, it was horseracing day, when we broadcast races live from Melbourne, Sydney and Brisbane. I had always found horseracing on the radio to be exceedingly boring, and now I was stuck with having to sit through it every Wednesday.

But I wondered... How often do those tipsters – Brian Martin, Johnny Tapp and Vince Curry – get it right? So I bought an exercise book, and every Wednesday I noted all the tips these guys gave at the start of the day, to see whether, if I had actually bet on the horses, I might win consistently. I did three charts – one as if I was betting for a win, one as if I was betting for a place, and one "each way". Now I was interested, as I listened to each race, to see whether "my" horses came in.

It turns out that if I had backed all the tips of one of the three tipsters for a place, I would have consistently made a profit. I never got into actual betting, but it gave me an interest, and allowed me to get through each Wednesday afternoon with a smile on my face.

Stay neutral

I spoke about this earlier, and I know this sounds very naïve, but it is more than ever necessary, epecially in a world where we have different versions of the truth, or "alternate facts". So forgive me if I harp on this one.

Over the past decade or so, several things have been happening to the way media work and the way people interpret media, and none of them are good.

With Trump, the media came in for a terrible beating in the USA. At the same time, mainstream media around the world have been swayed and polluted to the point that it is hard to get anything that sounds neutral. People listen to news THEY want to hear, told the way THEY want it told. The "Murdoch phenomenon" – in which one man, through his media, is able to influence countless millions of people into supporting certain political powers who, in turn, underpin those who support Murdoch, has metastasised and become a generalised cancer.

But Murdoch is certainly not the only one, and I am convinced he always worked the way he did because he saw an opportunity that wasn't there before. Globally, there are now countless examples of the same phenomena over and over again on both sides of the political gambit. And it goes further. A poll by CBS News / YouGov in Trump's third year of Presidency found that only 11% of Trump supporters trusted mainstream media, while 91% turned to the President for "accurate information". At a veterans' convention in July 2018, Trump drove it home, saying, *"Remember, what you are seeing and what you are reading is not what's happening"*. Remind you of something?

> *"The party told you to reject the evidence of your eyes and ears. It was their final, most essential command."*

Anyone who read George Orwell's 1984, may remember the chilling lines, *"The party told you to reject the evidence of your eyes and ears. It was their final, most essential command."* And Orwell went on, *"And if all others accepted the lie which the Party imposed —if all records told the same tale—then the lie passed into history and became truth. 'Who controls the past' ran the Party slogan, 'controls the future: who controls the present controls the past.'"*

And still further, *"In our age, there is no such thing as 'keeping out of politics'. All issues are political issues, and politics itself is a mass of lies, evasions, folly, hatred, and schizophrenia. When the general atmosphere is bad, language must suffer."*

"The goal eventually is the full destruction and elimination of the entire mainstream media," explained the ultra-right-wing Breitbart News Washington political editor, Matthew Boyle, speaking at an event for College conservatives at the Heritage

Foundation in July 2017. *"We envision a day when CNN is no longer in business. We envision a day when the New York Times closes its doors. I think that day is possible."*

In his speech, Boyle underlined Breitbart News' record in uncovering falsehoods reported in the mainstream media. Breitbart's fact-checking exposed a false CNN story that year. The story on CNN's website had claimed that President Trump's associate, Anthony Scaramucci (the "Mooch") – an import/export bank official formerly working at Goldman Sachs – was under investigation by the Treasury Department and Senate Intelligence Committee for alleged meetings with a Russian banking official. As it turned out, the supposed meetings never happened, and the Senate Intelligence Committee was not investigating.

Breitbart chirped about the fact that the CNN piece was entirely wrong, CNN retracted the piece, apologised to the offended party and three of its senior editorial staffers, including Pulitzer prize-winner Eric Lichtblau, resigned over the scandal.

Boyle argued that the failure of the mainstream media extended beyond a mere liberal bias. In his words: *"The media is an industry in crisis that refuses to admit that it's an industry in crisis. It's almost like an alcoholic refusing to admit that they have a problem. They continue to go out there and make the same mistakes over and over again. It's actually pretty easy, I could sit here all day and make a full time living on fact checking CNN. It gets boring after a while, but they make mistakes over and over again. Many of them, the same mistakes, and they refuse to correct them. Journalistic integrity is dead. There is no such thing anymore. So, everything is about 'weaponization of information'. Both sides are fighting on the battlefield of ideas and you know CNN, the New York Times, the Washington Post, Politico, Associated Press, MSNBC, NBC, CBS, the whole alphabet soup they've all thrown in together with the institutional left."*

Boyle explained that from his point of view, the key distinction between Breitbart and its "leftie" competition was that Breitbart admitted to being conservative. He said this contrasted with outlets of the "establishment" media that saw themselves as neutral and objective: *"They claim to be objective. They claim that they don't have a side. And many of them actually believe their own lies. So, a lot of these people are decent human beings who are working in a broken institution,"* he said.

Strangely, in all this, nothing was said of the highly influential and biased Fox News. Boyle speaks about outlets like Breitbart fighting against *"this behemoth of an industry that is all these different media organizations."*

Where Boyle has a point is in his organisation's ability to undermine the narrative of establishment media – to a certain extent. The victory of Donald Trump, whose candidacy received a record-low number of media endorsements, proved such success. But was it Breitbart, or was it simply Trump and his propaganda machine? I dare say it was more the latter.

What does this mean? To me, today's state of affairs is much more complex than anyone would like to admit. Yes, the mainstream media came under fire in the US – primarily by Trump himself, but also because they are not unbiased either. You might say, *"Well that's normal. Someone has to counter the right-wing rhetoric."*

Well, yes and no. Yes, it's important for people to get the "other side of the story". In an ideal world, the "perfect" media would present both sides "perfectly". But would that work in a world where there has been a total divergence of opinions, perpetuated by the media spin, in an accelerating dual spiral-dive – with very little or no middle ground remaining? People with liberal orientations only want to hear stories and opinions that comfort them and with which they agree entirely. And the same is true for the right.

So, can media really have an impact on the decision-making process of the public at large? Of course, they can, and do. While in the US, many of the mainstream media have taken a hit, most thinking people still peruse a range of media to get their ideas. In Europe, the media still tend, on the whole to be relatively more neutral in comparison to the divergence we see in the US.

This said, the UK is, and has for a long time, been a different animal, where the media are highly polarised and biased. Sadly, in my home country, Australia, the same is true today.

The more rhetoric that is put out there that the "mainstream media are dead", and so on, it's true that there will be an effect of *"When you throw enough mud, some of it will stick."* So, the mainstream media are taking a hit. But they're not not down for the count yet. The fact that in the US, it was Trump's hard-line followers who believed he was the messiah and everything he said and did was gospel didn't mean thinking people had disappeared from the surface of the earth.

We need to take the high ground – and stay there. Whoever you work for, your job IS to be as neutral as you can. While it is more popular to take sides, that is not your job. As I said before, you are not a commentator; you are a journalist. If you want to be a political commentator, that's fine, too, by the way. But it's a different job. The task of a good journalist is to reveal all facets of the story in such a way as to give people a good overall view. There is, of course, no such thing as *complete* neutrality, because there will always be elements that creep into a story that can give one or another side the edge. But work for the good stuff. Do your best.

Let me give you an example or two. In the section on press releases, I touch on the good relations I had with the National Party member Charles Blunt. I also mention the fact that our political views diverged totally. At the same time, the Federal candidates for the Liberal and Labor parties became great contacts, and even gave me references for the even-handed coverage I provided.

I was equally at ease when talking to Prime Ministers Malcolm Fraser (right), Bob Hawke (left), Paul Keating (left) or John Howard (right). There was never any political axe to grind. It was not the "Richard Barnes drags Howard over the coals" any more than sometimes I did with Bob Hawke. For news "grabs", good, or hard hitting questions are simply aimed at getting the answer you want. You are not "nice" to one and "mean" to another. If I had been able to complete my mission and talk to Saddam, it would have been the same.

The idea is to get a good interview or report that allows the audience to gain new insights into a story. In the mid-80s, there was also the dictatorial ultra-right-wing Premier of Queensland, Joh Bjelke Petersen, with whom I undertook a number of interviews. Face to face, he was very personable. After several meetings, I asked him, "What should I refer to you as, when we are talking? Mr Premier? Sir Joh?". He told me, *"Oh, goodness me, my boy. All my friends call me Joh. You call me Joh."*

This then put me into a rather funny situation the next time I called the Premier's office from the newsroom. The conversation went something like this:

"Hello, this is Richard Barnes calling from 4BC News. Could you put me through to the Premier please?"

"Let me check" – Puts me through. Premier picks-up phone – *"Hello… Richard – how are you?"*

"Hi Joh. Fine – just fine…"

At which point, the necks of five or six people in the newsroom turned to rubber, and all eyes turned towards me with a kind of incredulity. I can't really remember, but I guess

I was humored, even though this man was a blight on the state. He had gerrymandered the electorates to a point that even Trump would have been proud. He brought in crazy laws like "Disobeying a police directive" for which you could be jailed. It meant that if a police officer told you to stand on your head, and you didn't obey, you could be arrested.

That was Queensland in 1985. And yet, here was I chatting with this monster as though he was a normal guy. Because he was. Face to face, he was. That is, unless you were among those who rubbed him up the wrong way. In this case, my job was to get statements, and I didn't always ask "nice" questions.

There was one exception to my "neutrality" with political entities. It was in early 1986, when former Australian Prime Minister Gough Whitlam released an autobiography, and, as it turned out in my favour, his publicist was Jo Bramble, a lady I had worked with years before at radio 2LF in Young, and who had gone on to work for Penguin books. After he gave his press conference in Brisbane, she managed to get me a very nice "one on one" at his hotel (I was working at radio 4BC at the time). I must say that the strength of personality and aura of this man was such that I was just happy to talk to him. It must have shown. The highlight was when I asked him the simple question: *"How could you best describe the book?"*

"Well, the subject matter was very interesting, and it was particularly well written," he said. You have to imagine this with Gough's very particular way of speaking.

Indeed, the Prime Ministers could be quite humorous. Just as an anecdote, and nothing to do with any of this, the night I won the Pater Award in 1984, I was at the Press Club in Sydney, celebrating, when I followed the then Prime Minister, Bob Hawke into the Men's room. Coming out was John Laws – a legend of Australian radio – whom I had worked with when I was at 2UE two years hence (see earlier mention).

"This must be where the big knobs hang-out!", said Hawke.

It was so funny and apt at the time that I couldn't stop giggling for a very long time, especially as I was standing in there next to the trough...

I wonder if anywhere else in the world one could find a PM with the wit and presence of mind and timing to come up with something like that, in that situation, rather than nod and smile.

Don't let the stress get to you

Earlier on, I spoke about the importance of confidence and assertiveness. You may often find yourself not feeling confident at all on the inside. Stress is a very common disease among journalists. It could be said it comes with the trade. Thus, dealing with this stress is a key part of success as a journalist.

I learned this very early in my career; firstly, when I was at 2CC in Canberra, reading the news one afternoon. Our newsroom was open-plan, and the news "booth", from which we read the news, didn't have a door, but was semi-open to the newsroom. While the listeners couldn't hear what was going on, due to the fact we had a highly directional microphone, the person reading the news could well be disturbed by what was going on in the newsroom. On this day, there was a lot going on. I was about two minutes into my bulletin when my eyesight started going, from the outside in. It was as though I was in a tunnel that was closing-in on me as I read-on. I couldn't comprehend what was going on... just that I was little by little going blind. As the tunnel closed-in completely, I gave the prompt to the main studio – *"It's two minutes past three"* – their cue to throw to ads and the weather - much earlier than expected. I then stood up and turned around and announced to whoever was there that I couldn't see any more. I was driven home and a doctor came around to see me. I was starting, ever so slowly, to see again... but was quite concerned. Obviously. It turned out to be a kind of mental break-down from the stress. I had a couple of weeks off and was fine. I learned the importance of not trying to fight the feelings of stress, which only makes them worse... but to accept them and know that they are normal.

The next year, when I was working as a reporter and evening / weekend news presenter on 2WS in Sydney, something similar happened, only this time, not to me. Our key afternoon news reader was the highly popular Canadian, Pat Thorogood. One day, while I was working as a reporter – gathering and writing news, the bulletin at the top of the hour just "stopped" half way through. Pat had passed-out in the news booth. The on-air presenter ran a couple of ads, and as Pat was pulled out of the booth, I was asked to go in and replace him and finish reading the news. I was thus, at age 21, probably the youngest news presenter on prime afternoon radio in Sydney – every day for a couple of weeks, until Pat got better.

As time has passed, there have been various episodes when stress has been an issue. In March, 1990, I was asked to be the MC for the "Australian Rock Night" at the Midem Festival in Cannes. Being an Aussie, working in radio and TV at the time on the French Riviera, I "fit the bill". The show was to be held in the main hall of the Palais des Festivals – the same venue as the famed Film Festival – with a live audience of around 1,500 in the hall, and with the whole thing televised live on an Australian TV channel. My job was to present the show – with a number of big name Australian acts, talk about the sponsors, and do the kind of things an MC usually does. The rehearsals took place in the early afternoon. They basically just needed me to know where I had to stand and get the scripts for what I had to say. As MC, I would walk out at exactly the right moment, stand centre stage, and present the show.

"What lighting will there be?", I asked.

"*A single spotlight,*" was the answer.

Hmmmm. I had a lot of notes to read, with lists of sponsors and so on.

"*I may be semi-blinded by the light,*" I suggested. "*Is there another light above me you could put on as well, so I can read the notes?*"

The answer was affirmative, and I went about my way in town until the show was about to start. My wife was there, in the audience.

As the event was to be televised live, the start time was exact, with a countdown. Around one minute from show-time, I asked, "*So everything is fine with the lights?*"

"*Yes, the spotlight is working fine,*" said an assistant.

"*No... I mean the other light, so I can see what I'm reading.*"

"*There's just a spotlight,*" she said... Followed by another voice saying "*Thirty seconds. Standing-by.*"

"*What if I can't read the text?*" I asked.

"*Do you want a flashlight?*", she asked.

"*Yeah, sure. I go walking on the stage with a flashlight in my hand. Leave it... Holy shit.*"

"*Ten seconds...*"

A hand was on my shoulder as the final countdown was completed. I was shaking like a leaf, and really felt like I was going to pass out... "*Three, two one... We're live.*"

I bounded onto the stage, and took place centre stage as the intro music died down. Thankfully, the spotlight was high enough that I could see the notes. I was still shaking and felt terrible, but launched into it with full gusto. I announced the show, all the sponsors, and the first act, and breezed off the stage. I had survived.

As the first act was nearing its end, the manager of the second act – Joe Camilleri – a very well-known Australian singer – famous for his group Jo Jo Zep and the Falcons (among others) – approached me backstage.

"Jo is always a bit nervous before performing," he explained. *"Please keep his intro as short as possible. He prefers that."*

Hey. I thought I had been the nervous one. *"Of course,"* I said in my ultra-confident presenter voice. *"Tell him not to worry."*

In September, 1999, I was taken on as the "media guy" for Monaco's Pro-Celebrity golf tournament, "starring", among others, Kevin Costner, who, by the way, won the amateur prize. There was a whole swathe of stars there, including Gary Player, Christopher Lee, Tico Torres, Robert Wagner, Roger Moore, Lance Armstrong, Henri Leconte, Boris Becker, Alberto Tomba… and of course, Prince Albert… the list goes on. The tournament finished with a gala evening at the Monte Carlo Sporting Club, and I was the MC.

At one point, I called Kevin Costner to the stage, as on my script, he was listed as giving a speech and prize. When he arrived on the stage, Prince Albert was still addressing the audience, and Kevin whispered to me, *"No one asked me to give a speech. You have to get someone else."*

I sent someone to get Roger Moore, and Costner just presented a prize, without giving a longer talk.

"Have you had time to have something to eat?", I asked Moore.

"Yes," he slurred. *"And I have had time to have something to drink as well."* … Oops. This might not have been a good idea.

When Moore took to the microphone, he gave a wonderful, beautifully crafted speech about his charity, and about the event.

No one could have been more eloquent. Wow. I was in awe. Moore's way of speaking... his diction and tone... were superb.

Afterwards, I was puzzled by how he remembered such a long speech, and asked him about it. *"I guess you are used to memorising lines after all these years. My dad was an actor, and I know how much work it can be,"* I said. *"But what happens if you forget your lines – there on the stage in front of thousands of people?",* I asked.

"Oh, there are two things you can do in that case," said Moore. *"You can either burst into tears or faint, and I prefer the latter, because you get to lie down for a while."*

There's no doubt that Roger Moore was witty not only on-screen, but in real life as well.

The next year, I was again involved with the Pro-Celebrity golf event, and this time, the gala dinner was at the Yacht Club, where again I was MC. I happened to be seated not far from Kevin Costner, so I said *"Oh Kevin, I'll get you to come and speak in a minute",* as a bit of a joke.

"Noooo..." he said. *"I haven't prepared anything."*

I told him it was just a gag and that he didn't have to speak. After this, Kevin explained to me why he didn't want to talk the previous year, explaining it was simply because he has a strong need to prepare for such things - not to be "thrown into it".

Of course. Not everyone has the same approach to acting or presenting. Costner had also been upset when someone photographed him getting out of the helicopter – arriving in Monaco. He was jetlagged, had bags under his eyes, and was not in top shape. As one of the world's most famed actors, image counts. It really counts. If you sputter or hesitate in front of thousands of people at a gala because you have not prepared for a talk, it's not OK. He needed to be prepared. Of course, I understood. Costner told me he thought I looked at ease on the stage, and I took that as a huge complement.

The best advice is "fake it 'till you make it". When you start out in a lot of this stuff, you may be very stressed. Just let it go, and accept that it is normal. The more you try to fight it, the worse it will be. Know that even the top professionals in the industry get stressed. In any case, the more you practice your art, the more you will gain confidence in yourself.

I was listening to Dan Rather, in his audiobook version of "Rather Outspoken", as he described how it was to be the live TV anchor as the 9/11 drama was unfolding in New York. He outlines just how hard it was not to show his stress and emotion at a time like that, despite being one of the most experienced anchors of all time. A week or so later, when Rather was being interviewed in turn on a talk show – going back over the horrors of that day, he broke down. All that pent-up stress found an escape valve. Rather said he was not at all embarrassed by this. It would be fair to say that the opposite reaction – having a cold, external view of something so enormous, tragic and horrific – would have been unusual.

Indeed, being a news journalist can harden you to many things. But there is a limit.

MY EARLY DAYS

A bit about myself... I grew up as the son of a TV and film actor dad, and a ceramicist mum, whose artistic stroke was no doubt inherited in turn from her landscape artist mum.

Until I was eight, we lived in Sydney's northern suburbs. Then we moved to the ghost mining town of Sunny Corner between Bathurst and Lithgow – around 200 km west of Sydney, on the other side of the Blue Mountains. A lot of the time, dad would be off acting, primarily in Melbourne, where he would work on Crawford Productions TV shows like Matlock Police, Division 4 or Homicide. Dad had started out in radio in the 1940s, working on 3DB in Melbourne, presenting Australia's first "hit parade", when radio presenters used to dress in dinner suits. He was described in one book as "the best-known voice on Australian radio", due to his very regular participation in the radio drama series of the 1950s and early 60s produced by Grace Gibson Radio Productions in Sydney.

Dad's three brothers all worked in radio as well. Jack worked at 2UW in Sydney as programme manager, and was also secretary of Actors' Equity for some time. Uncle Bill worked at a station in Alice Springs and Keith at a station in Portland, Victoria. It was a family thing. One of dad's brothers worked for a while as an office boy for Sir Frank Packer – a powerful media magnate – who owned the Daily Telegraph (sold later to Murdoch). He had one funny anecdote of when my uncle was in Packer's office and overheard his secretary telling him the Prime Minister was there to see him, to which he replied, *"He doesn't have an appointment. Tell him to wait."* Says something of the power of the media at the time.

Dad worked on the stage in New Guinea during the war, in London in the 50's, and back in Sydney in the late 50's and 60's, before going on primarily to work for TV and film as an actor in the 70s and 80s. Of course, there was a bit of cross-over, as dad's first films were shot in the 1950s (i.e. Carrington V.C., Siege of Pinchgut, and Summer of the 17th Doll). For those who lived through the 70's in Australia, his face and voice were very familiar through series like Homicide, Division 4, Matlock, Number 96, Silent Number, Skippy, Boney, the People Next Door, A Country Practice... and films like White Man's Legend, Stone, The Man from Hong Kong, The Hands of Cormack Joyce, The Cars that Ate Paris... the list goes on.

When I was at school, people would ask if I wanted to be an actor like my dad, and I would very clearly say no. I wanted to be a marine biologist. I'd seen ALL the Jacques Cousteau films, I loved diving, and thought that kind of life looked pretty amazing. And being an actor meant being away from home all the time, or being depressed if you were at home, as it meant you weren't on-location, working.

At age 17, I obtained my Higher School Certificate at All Saints' College in Bathurst, going to the college for the last two years after spending the first four primarily at Bathurst High School (except for a 6-month respite when we all moved down to Sydney as dad had a full-time role in a series, and it was easier for us all to be down there than for him to commute). At the end of January 1978, I packed my belongings into my car and drove the 300km to Newcastle, on the coast, with the aim of eventually getting a science degree and becoming a marine biologist.

To make a bit of extra money, I managed to get a part time

job at the commercial radio station 2KO, screening calls and occasionally doing panel operating for a morning "open-line" show hosted by Tim Webster and Matt Tapp. Then, as disillusion set-in with the studies (chemistry, geology and uni-level maths were, it turns out, not my bag – at all ... and even biology was a drag), I amused myself by starting a show on the university FM station – 2NUR-FM.

This was not "getting into" radio. It was just having fun, right? Right?

The station manager named the show "Super Rock". Ughhh. That lasted a month. Then I noticed that in the official programme book, the names of shows were written in big capital letters, while the details were in small type. I realised that if I gave a very long name to my show, it was stand out from all the rest. So, I changed the show's name to "Vesuvian Vibes from the Mythical Magical Mouse Munching Machine". I also figured that if the name was crazy and ambiguous enough, it would arouse even more curiosity. I don't know if it did or not, as not many people called, if any. It was during my stint at 2NUR-FM that I did my first interview – with David Briggs, the lead guitarist of Little River Band. What a talent, and no doubt very understanding to take an 18-year-old university radio guy seriously. I gather he probably didn't ever know the NAME of my show or he would have run straight out the door, with the absolute conviction that I was a weirdo.

As dad had a huge background in radio, I asked him to listen to one of my shows and give me some tips on how to do it better. He listened, and told me, *"Just keep at it. Keep practicing, and you'll be OK"*. That WASN'T what I wanted to hear. I was expecting some kind of detailed explanation about the finesse of attacking phrases with the right intonations and so on. I figure he probably felt there was so much work to do that he didn't know where to start. As I learned later, doing air-checks – in other words, recording yourself and listening back to your broadcast – is an extremely important exercise. It's essential to growing as a presenter.

I failed all my subjects at uni except biology, and dropped-out after the first year, returning, with tail between legs, to my parents' place at Sunny Corner. I quickly landed a job selling menswear at Myer Bathurst – a big department store. Some might sneer, but it was there that I learned my very valuable lesson about selling points and customer benefits (see also section on this), that I have been able to apply in recent years in commercial journalism. I was quick also to get a weekend radio show up and running at 2MCE-FM – the local college station. I didn't give it a way-out name, but I did start to get phone calls from listeners who liked the music, which was very much influenced by my then brother-in-law, John, a Canadian with highly eclectic musical tastes, not to mention my now being in a new-wave cum punk band called the "Septic Tanks", which went on to do much better things under different names, including Pneumatic Swing Inc – or PSI – and whose more talented members still regularly play today (I played lead guitar).

After eight months at Myers, realising selling men's clothing was not my thing, even though apparently, I was good at it, I asked Ron Camplin, owner of 2BS Bathurst and a few other stations, if he didn't have any jobs going. Ron was a family friend, and my mother had even worked for him years before, scheduling ads.

While I was still at Myers, Ron gave me a job on the Saturday afternoon horse racing show. It simply meant playing ads in the breaks – so panel operating – which I knew how to do by now. I found horse racing on radio terribly boring, but at the end of the day, after the races, I had the chance to place some music… to be a "DJ" – for around an hour – up to 6pm. It was a foot in the door, and the last hour made all the rest worth it.

After a few weeks, Ron pulled me to one side. *"I like what I hear"*, he said. *"Do you want a full-time job? I have an opening at 2LF, Young, as afternoon presenter."*

Holy Moly. The money was just as crappy as what I was getting at Myers, and Young was a tiny town in the middle of nowhere. But it was a real radio DJ job at a real commercial station. I leapt at it, of course.

I was instantly absorbed by my work. Being afternoon presenter meant playing music and occasionally talking about stuff from 2pm to 6pm, while the rest of the day was taken up by making ads – something you can get addicted to, as the creative process is a lot of fun. I did a huge amount of free overtime, amusing myself in this way. One time, the only news journalist at the station was off for a week or so, and I had to replace him doing the local bulletins. I found it very interesting.

In June 1980, after having worked at 2LF for around ten months, Ron Camplin called me and told me he'd booked me for a weekend radio workshop in Canberra, covering copywriting, news, presenting style and so on. At the workshop, the news section was run by Greg Milne – News Director from 2WS in Sydney, and author of "The Radio Journalist". At the end of the weekend, Greg told me I could get a job as a cadet journalist in a big station, and asked if I was interested. I said I didn't know. How could I shaft Ron Camplin who just sent me to this workshop? The next day, when I was back on the job in Young, Milne called me and said the job was at 2CC Canberra.

I called Ron... embarrassed. *"Take it. Don't hesitate a second,"* said Ron. I was flabbergasted. He had given me my first chance in commercial radio, had paid for me to go to a weekend workshop, and he gave me his blessing to leave? He explained that this was the way the business worked.

As it turns out, Ron Camplin doubtless gave more people a first chance in radio than anyone else in Australia over the years; many of whom went on to great things. He also gave chances to people with handicaps that otherwise would have precluded them from careers in radio. One was blind, meaning all scripts had to be in Braille, and another had no arms, using his feet to operate the panel (we didn't have separate panel operators). That was when I was still a teenager when my mother was working at the station – and I used to sit in with the presenter watching how he worked. It was a revelation. I am convinced that at the time, no other radio boss would have given these guys a chance, as they fit into the "too hard" basket. Ron was different.

So off I went to Canberra, where I debuted my career as a radio journalist. After less than a year at 2CC, Greg Milne called me back – this time with a job at 2WS, under his management – beginning May 1981. 2WS was only a couple of years old – WS meaning "West Sydney".

At first, 2WS targeted people in Western Sydney, but when I arrived, it was going for a broader listenership – primarily 18-35-year-olds – with a format of "Greatest Memories and Latest Hits". While the station overall was probably number four or five in the ratings, we were number one in that particular demographic across Sydney. This demographic also happened to be that of the biggest spenders, so the station was successful. The news team was highly competent, and news was an important part of the programming – as was sport on the weekends. The atmosphere was very professional, but still a little relaxed. We even had a "rec" room with a space invaders machine and where we had Friday evening get-togethers. Greg Milne would regularly involve himself in giving tips to all the journalists. Of course, the best training was seeing each story "marked up" by the desk editors. And they were bloody good.

Then, after a little under a year, I learned a lesson the hard way about the effect of ratings on stations in a highly competitive market like Sydney. 2WS had dropped in the ratings, meaning a bunch of advertisers pulled out. Consequentially, the budget for the news staff took a major blow. Milne actually had tears in his eyes as he let me go, along with a couple of other people. I was more dispensable, as I was less polyvalent – not being apt to do football reports on the weekends – just news – so those who could multitask got to stay. Yes, Milne was very upset. But he was also very proactive in helping me move on. It was thanks to his call to Mark Collier, Director of News and Public Affairs at 2UE – the then overall number one station in Sydney – that I went on to take a job there in July, 1982.

2UE was another exceptional training ground – and has always been a legendary station. Based in North Sydney, we had a "news/talk" format, and presenters included the legendary John Laws, Gary O'Callaghan and John Pearce. Our news service was the heart of the Australia-wide "United Network", and was networked to around 50 provincial stations. The 2UE news style guide was several hundred pages long – covering everything you could possibly want to know about the job. One was handed this "bible" with the understanding that if you did something contrary to what was decreed within, you would have your arse kicked to kingdom come. I still have the style guide today, and it even inspired part of the content of this book. Everything at 2UE news was very matter-of-fact and serious. We were an affiliate of CBS Radio News in the US – exchanging reports with them as news happened.

But while 2UE was an incredible place to learn, the hours and shifts drove me crazy. In Australian radio news, the breakfast shift generally starts at 4am. By 5, the first bulletin goes on air, then it's every half hour until at least nine o'clock. It means getting up before 3am in order to get to work on time. Even if the shift is regular, you never get used to it.

One important lesson at 2UE was in fact about getting to work on time. One morning, I woke up a little after 4am with the phone ringing. It was one of my colleagues… *"Where the fuck are you?"*

My electric alarm clock was flashing zero on and off. Evidently, I had had a power blackout during the night. I leapt into clothes and got into the newsroom around 4:45. Not being there in those critical first moments of the shift, when the workload was very heavy – gathering everything we needed for the first bulletins – put everyone else in the shit. When Mark came in at 9am, he pulled me off to one side and said, *"Next time your alarm doesn't go off, you can stay in bed."*

Message received. I made sure I had two different alarms – one which was battery powered. Since that day I was never late for a shift again. Ever.

At 2UE, every week was the same mish-mash: 4am 'till midday on Wednesday and Thursday, 9am 'till 5pm on Friday, and 3pm 'till midnight on Saturday and Sunday. Monday and Tuesday off, then the same again. For a few weeks, it's OK... but it's like being constantly jetlagged. And no weekends.

After 10 months, and continuing promises from the bosses that shifts would get better, it was too much. I heard there was a job going down the road at 2SM – "The Rock of the 80's" – just doing breakfast shifts Monday through Friday. Weekends off! 2UE was number one in Sydney and 2SM was quite a way down the list. The news "cred" of 2SM was not the same – as the target was 18–25-year-olds (where in fact the station held the #1 spot), and there were only three others working in the newsroom.

I would be reading "network-only" news (just going out to the small regional network of 2SM – way smaller than 2UE) from 5 'till 9 – while on 2SM, at the same time, it was the legendary (late) Jim Angel, and then I would be on 2SM news 'till midday. I jumped at the chance. I loved the rock'n'roll atmosphere at 2SM, and the views from our newsroom over Sydney harbour – the bridge and the opera house – were incredible. "Little" Jimmy was a great bloke to work with, as was Andrew Vickery – the "other" news guy – also senior to me – a very funny bloke indeed. I always thought it was very amusing that 2SM – owned by the church – the SM meaning "Saint Mark's" – had newsmen called Vickery and Angel. Strange how names go.

For its target group, 2SM was quite legendary. The first time I got a hint of this was when there was a school group visiting the station and one of the kids asked me, *"What's it like being famous?"*

I told him I was just a news guy... but he insisted... *"But I hear you on the radio every day. That's famous".* So, I guess for him I was. Perception is a funny thing.

At 2SM, I developed – for the time I was there – a new feature: music industry news. I figured the audience would be more interested in the comings and goings of the music industry than a lot of the other stuff we were talking about in "general" news. I contacted all the music companies the station worked with, and it turned out to be a nice weekly spot – with a good following.

But after around eight or nine months, I fell prey to the same problem as I had back at 2WS. Ratings went down and, yes, they had to shed staff. During my notice period, I discovered the fact that 2LM Lismore – in northern New South Wales – was looking for someone to start a regional news service for them, right from scratch. The idea was extremely appealing, as I love the Northern Rivers area and spent a lot of time at Byron Bay during my younger years... so I applied. I flew up to Lismore to meet the management of the station – owned by the Northern Star newspaper group. Their on-air presenters had, until this time, simply read-out the regional news from the newspaper. Not really what radio is meant for – i.e. immediacy. I landed the job, primarily, it turns out, because my news director at 2SM gave a shining reference.

I arrived to a bare office, which I had to equip from top to toe, and had one other person to help – Ian Richards – who did the mid-morning programme on air, and would run the afternoon news – while I would be News Director and morning newsman. Ian was an accomplished journalist and he also had a great voice.

I established a wide range of close contacts within the police, fire brigade, local councils, political spheres and so on, and decided to set myself a goal: to one day win the Pater Award for best regional news in Australasia. Back then, the Pater Awards were the national recognition for professional excellence. After less than a year of operation, in 1984, we pitched for the awards – with a general presentation about our news service, and another one about our coverage of the young people who were kicked off the dole because they went to college part time to try to better themselves (I talked about that earlier). I was called to travel to the gala event in Sydney for the awards, as we had made it into the finals. At the awards ceremony, I almost fell off my chair when they announced 2LM had won the prize for the best regional news in Australasia. Bugger. It had been my goal… Now what?

Ita Buttrose – when she handed me the award said, *"You won the award in the very first year of your news service. What do you do for an encore?"*

"I'll just have to do it again". The answer sounded hollow. It was like any major goal, once you've made it, you need to have another one to move on towards. But I didn't. At the ceremony, I was also blown away by the fact that we had made it to the finals in the "Best Single Event News" category – for our story about the students.

There was, of course, a big celebration at the station. A magnum of Bollinger Champagne was cracked open by Steve, the station manager, and the Pater win was largely promoted in the press. My obvious first request to the boss was, *"How about a raise?"*

It was explained to me that a raise was not on the books. At the same time, in Brisbane, radio 4BC, another affiliate of the

United Network, was looking for a breakfast news desk editor and all-round reporter. I went to see news director Ray Rigby... and to cut a long story short, the job was mine.

I had just turned 25 as I started my job in Brisbane, running the busiest news shift at an important all news/talk station. We had a "double-header" news presentation in the mornings, with Cameron Bond and Glenn Taylor. Taylor at the time was also well known for presenting the magazine shows and evening news on TV, and while he added a bit of pizzazz to the line-up, he was only a presenter, not a writer, as virtually all other radio news presenters are. Cameron was a wonderfully flamboyant gay man at a time when it was less common for gays to be open about their sexuality. In the years following my working with him, he sadly died in a motorbike crash.

My job was to manage the news team, dealing out the jobs, and assembling each bulletin to go to air. While the task was not difficult in itself, my young age made it very tough telling longer-in-the-tooth journalists what to do. While I was at 4BC, we did manage to win the Pater Award for best news in Australasia with our "two-man show". To add a little spice to my working days at 4BC, I came up with the idea of doing weekly motoring reports – testing cars and reporting on their pros and cons. I contacted all the car manufacturers, and they were all happy to give me a different car every week in return for the reports. One of the journalists asked me why I, who had no experience testing cars, was doing this. I replied simply that I was the one who had the idea. Simple really.

After a while at 4BC, I realised that the only way I could move up in the business would be to go into management; which I didn't want to do. I was at a bit of a crossroads.

In March, 1986, my mother called me and told me that the colon cancer my grandmother had developed had generalised, and that I should come down to see her at a hospital in Bathurst.

Driving from Brisbane would have taken around 12 hours, so I flew to Sydney, rented a car and drove up to Bathurst.

I saw my grandmother in hospital, dying the kind of death people do from that cursed affliction: one where all your dignity is taken away. I drove back to Sydney and had dinner at the Oaks pub in Neutral Bay with my former colleague, Maybritt. She had been sales secretary at 2SM and we'd become close friends while I was there. She told me she was planning to do a five or six month "big Europe trip" – a thing many of us Aussies do – and intimated she wouldn't mind having some extra company.

My notice was on my boss's table the next morning in Brisbane. That's how the whole "Europe thing" started, beginning with a flight from Sydney to Athens on the 5th of May, 1986.

While Maybritt stayed on longer in the Greek islands, having met a man running a hotel on Corfu (very convenient!), I continued on through Yugoslavia, Italy, France and the UK, looking for a bit of odd work after months of travel. I reported for Australian radio from the Commonwealth Games in Edinburgh, and worked part time for a couple of months at Capital Radio in London – doing reports for a programme called "The Way It Is".

I finally ended up staying in Europe, having met Fabienne – my wonderful, patient and thankfully very supportive French wife – and mother of my two beautiful (now grown-up) girls, on the beach in Ventimiglia, on the Italian Riviera. It was here that I had found some work at Riviera 104 - an English language station broadcasting across the border over the Côte d'Azur. The station went on to be called Riviera Radio, having moved to Monaco.

I gave up my ticket home and settled with Fabienne in Menton on the Côte d'Azur – just next to the Italian border.

Riviera Radio would take-up seven years of my life – during which I first worked in programmes, but then, primarily in advertising.

I also worked in TV – producing and presenting a weekly magazine show on TMC in Monaco, and presenting another one for NBC Superchannel produced by World Magazine, before creating my own media consultancy, and launching into the world of print media in the late 90's, moving away from Menton to Saint Laurent du Var – just next to Nice.

I also worked in the late 90's as a part-time professor of communications and marketing at IUT Sophia Antipolis – part of Nice University, and another highlight was being in charge of the translation team for official press releases from the FIFA World Cup Soccer in France in 1998 at the Marseille site.

From 2000 up until the Covid crisis, I primarily worked for the Cleverdis media group in France, in the field of commercial journalism, consulting and analysis. I was editor-in-chief for virtually all their publications from their beginnings.

The lessons that I could relate from my younger days are:

- When starting out in the business, be willing to do stuff for free if you like it and if you can learn from it.

- Follow your instinct and "take a leap" of faith if you think something is worth it.

- Apply yourself to being highly creative and different in your work.

- Don't take anything personally. I've been retrenched by people I considered good friends, who had no choice – and - I have had to let people go whom I considered good friends when I was in management.

- Work hard when you have to. Bloody hard, and always do more than you're paid for. Go the extra mile – every day.

BIBLIOGRAPHY

Associated Press Style Book and Libel Manual: https://www.apstylebook.com/

Australian Film, Television and Radio School: various course notes: https://www.aftrs.edu.au/

BBC Academy: https://www.bbc.co.uk/academy/en

Cappon, Rene: Associated Press Guide to News Writing

Carnegie, Dale: How to Win Friends and Influence People

CBS News Style Guide: https://www.cbs.dk/files/cbs.dk/dcosta_contributor_style_guide.pdf

Cole, Peter: How to Write – Newswriting https://www.theguardian.com/books/2008/sep/25/writing.journalism.news

Encyclopaedia Britannica: https://www.britannica.com/

Evans, Harold: Essential English for Journalists, Editors and Writers (fully revised edition)

Federal Bureau of Investigation: Elicitation Techniques - https://www.fbi.gov/file-repository/elicitation-brochure.pdf/view

King, Stephen: On Writing; a Memoir of the Craft

Milne, Greg: The Radio Journalist – a Guide to Radio News

Pirsig, Robert M.: Zen and the Art of Motorcycle Maintenance

Rankmath: https://rankmath.com/blog/power-words/

Rather, Dan: Rather Outspoken – My Life in the News (Digby Diehl)

Schafer Jack, Ph.D. and Karling, Marvin, Ph.D.: The Like Switch

Strunk Jr, William and E. B. White: The Elements of Style – 4th Edition

The Economist: Style Guide – 12th edition

Waterhouse, Keith: On Newspaper Style

Wikipedia: https://www.wikipedia.org/

Printed in Great Britain
by Amazon

23118057R00106